Vision from the Heart

By

Gary Haun

ISBN: 1-4033-2220-1 (e-book)
ISBN: 1-4033-2221-X (Paperback)
ISBN: 1-4107-3918-X (Dust Jacket)

This book is printed on acid free paper.

1st Books - rev. 6/11/03

Dedication

In the days of old, the sea captains were comforted by the sight of the lanterns in the lighthouses. It meant safety and helped them as they ventured along the rocky shores.
Life, like the waters of the ocean, has many days with rough seas and uncharted waters. We must all look to the lighthouses in our lives.
My lighthouse has been, and always will be, my son, Billy.

Photography by Roger Kyler

I think of Roger as a brother. Like a

guardian angel, he has watched over me,

from the snow-covered summit of

Mount Kilimanjaro to the sandy floor

of the ocean.

From shark-diving to skydiving, or

manatees to mountains, Roger has been

beside me. I wish everyone could have

a friend like Rog.

Introduction

As we journey through life we meet all manner of people. We often pass each other by without a glance, two ships passing in the night. Or we may stop to pass the time of day, exchanging ideas and smiles. Occasionally though, we meet someone who makes such a profound impact that we can never forget that person, with whom we establish a lasting relationship. One such person, for me, is Gary Haun.

I still remember the first letter I received from him. Across the top of the letterhead I read "The Amazing Haundini," and there was a picture of a magician's top hat complete with wand, white rabbit, and playing card. The writer of the letter asked if I would send him an autographed photo that he could put up on his office wall. Well, that was an easy enough request to fulfill. He went on to tell me he was a magician and then—as a sort of afterthought—came a comment that the writer was 100% blind.

I did a double take. It was amazing that a blind man should be a magician. But why would he want an autographed photo, that he could not see, to put on his office wall? I did not know Gary then, as I know him now. I did not know how his indomitable spirit had refused to allow his blindness to destroy his love of life, his love of his fellow men, his ability to accomplish whatever he sets his mind to, and to do it at least as well as others do, and often better.

I sent him his photo. I also wrote a long letter. I told him about our program for young people, Roots and Shoots. I explained how I always encouraged youngsters to search for real life heroes. Heroes, like Gary Haun. I asked him if he would become involved in Roots and Shoots, and help us establish clubs in the schools where he did his magic. Those two letters, his to me and my reply, marked the beginning of our friendship.

It was not for another year or so that I would meet Gary. We invited him to one of our Roots and Shoots summits—some 45 young people gathered together from across North America for three days of shared environmental and community activities, journaling, and fun. I was out with the group when Gary arrived with his friend Roger

Kyler. He walked on Roger's arm, barely using his slender, lightweight, telescoping cane. He wore flamboyant clothes—boots with black coat and trousers, white frilled shirt, black bow tie, black, broad-brimmed magicians hat, and very black, dark glasses. He shook hands. How could he shake hands without fumbling? As he talked, he looked directly into my eyes. How could he look, or seem to look, into my eyes? All this will be revealed in *Vision From the Heart*.

I have learned so much from Gary. I have sensed, through his mind, and above all from his heart, something of his world of darkness—a world that is lit by his dynamic spirit, his absolute refusal to be defeated. This book describes all that he has accomplished without the use of his eyes—without the ability to use what we sighted people take so much for granted. And his accomplishments are truly astounding. But it is the little everyday things that I find just as inspirational. Like the telephone call I received last spring. His voice came over the line loud and clear. "Jane, I wish you were here today. The sun's shining, and there's a mother duck out on the river, with her little ducklings all bobbing along behind. The cutest thing you ever saw." I was fascinated, for we shared a picture of sunshine, water, and ducks that neither of us could actually see.

Then there was the time when I had a little get-together in my hotel room, just a small group of friends, including Gary and Roger. Mary Lewis, my executive assistant and best of friends, was sitting on the floor and quietly working on some papers while the rest of us talked and drank scotch. Suddenly Gary turned to Mary, "It's time you stopped working," he said, "You need a scotch." Mary's face was a study as she stared at this magic man who was blind but knew exactly where she was and knew she was working. This is why, for much of the time, it's hard to remember that Gary cannot see. He is an inspiration because he has overcome his blindness with such determination, such indomitable will power.

He is also an inspiration because he does so much for other people. Here's another story. It began with a talk I gave at a school in New Jersey. Of course, my mascot, Mister H, was with me—the peculiar-looking monkey that Gary gave me four years ago for one of my birthdays, thinking it was a chimpanzee. And, as usual, I introduced Mister H to the kids and told them about the indomitable spirit of the man who had given him to me. After the lecture the headmaster asked if Mister H could be taken over to a little boy of eight years who had just become blind. When I went to meet the child and his mother I could sense the fear and the despair in both. They had only recently arrived in the area and seemed to have no one to help them in this nightmare time. The child did not raise his head. I talked to them for a while. Later, I called Gary, and with the help of the headmaster, we arranged a time when we could call the family. That call transformed their lives. He told the mother of all the different services—and fun things—available to the blind. Then he talked to the child. Later, his mother told the headmaster how her boy had held his head high and said, "That man said he could teach me to scuba dive, and do judo. And that I would do it better than lots of other boys. He said it doesn't matter being blind. He's blind too." For the first time in weeks he was smiling and happy.

All that took place in November. "I didn't think I could get through Thanksgiving this year," the mother told the headmaster. "But now I can celebrate along with everyone else."

"Take Mister H with you on your travels," Gary had said. "Then you'll know I'm with you in spirit." Mister H has been with me to 34 countries, to some of them many times. I've introduced him at hundreds of lectures, dinner parties and other gatherings. And through Mister H, the story of the amazing blind magician has inspired thousands of people in all corners of the globe. I tell people that if they touch him they will never be the same again, "For something of the indomitable spirit of Gary Haun is somehow captured in this funny little person." Even funnier now, for Mister H has changed shape, color and texture since he was presented to me—he must have been touched, squeezed, kissed, stroked and hugged by well over 300,000 people! And all of them, adults and children alike, along with thousands who had no chance to touch Mister H, were inspired by the story of Gary Haun.

Now thousands more will be inspired by this remarkable book about one of the most remarkable men I have met. *Vision From the Heart* is a true-life story of a true-life hero—one of my reasons for hope—hope for the future of our human species on planet Earth.

Dr. Jane Goodall

Prologue

Gary Haun was born on the 4th of July. At the age of 17, he enlisted in the United States Marine Corps. He achieved the rank of sergeant and was a hydraulics technician in a helicopter squadron. In July 1973, while working on a helicopter, a hydraulic line burst open and blinded both his eyes. The Navy doctors told Sgt. Haun that the blindness was permanent and that there was no operation or cure that would help.

After being retired from the Marine Corps, Gary would begin a new journey down many different paths. His perspective on adjusting to and accepting challenges is the basis of this book.

As the Amazing Haundini, Gary has performed magic for thousands of people. His real magic, however, is inspiring people to look within themselves for the strength to overcome life's challenges. This book is not about sight, but insight.

Let Gary take you beyond your limits. After reading this book, you may not have the desire to swim with sharks or go skydiving...it's only important that you have desire. This book is not about living with blindness, it's about living.

Chapter 1

"If you raise your children to feel they can accomplish any goal or task they decide upon, you will have succeeded as parents, and you will have given your children the greatest of all blessings."

—*Brian Tracy*

The Adventure Begins...

I was born on July the Fourth, 1952. To this day, I think there is a parallel between my birth date and my character. July 4th is Independence Day, the birth of the United States of America. I suppose it is not a matter of coincidence that I have such a strong belief in the independence of the human spirit.

When I was just a baby, my mother tied small metal bells to my baby shoes. "He always had a sense of adventure," she would say. The bells were to alert her to my whereabouts. As we lived in a two-story apartment building, my mother was afraid of me falling from the open balcony. I was always trying to find a way out through the locked door. I suspect, in some Freudian way, this would later be my reason for my interest in learning escape technology as it relates to magic.

My family was not wealthy. Please let me clarify that. We did not have an abundance of money. However, we were wealthy in another aspect. I always felt loved as a child and can never remember going without. It has been said that a rich man is he who wants little. I do remember as a small child being given cardboard boxes to play with. I was completely fascinated with them. I had a particular fondness for the round Quaker Oatmeal boxes. I would find them a very versatile toy. One day the oatmeal box might serve as a barn silo next to the shoe box farmhouse. On another day, it might serve as a portable marble box. I suppose those boxes would not hold the interest of today's children. With talking electronic dogs, video games, and remote control cars, the oatmeal box does seem a bit out of place. But then again, a child being perfectly happy with a cardboard box seems out of place in today's modern society.

One of the fondest memories of my childhood is that of my cat Sparky and my dog Blackie. There is no doubt in my mind that they were the best cat and dog in the world. Sparky was an orange-and-white tabby cat. He was my best friend. I would lie down on the floor and Sparky would crawl up on my back and go to sleep. I thought that was the neatest thing in the world. He would be so content that he would snore.

He also loved to play. I would tie something on a string and pull it through the house, and Sparky would pounce upon the string and roll around on it. At Christmas time, Sparky would sit for hours and watch the twinkling of the Christmas tree lights. Then he would see his reflection in one of the ornaments and swat at it. When he was tired, he would crawl under the tree for a nap. I think I will always remember him lying underneath the Christmas tree. He was a happy cat, and he made others feel happy. I suppose that's what childhood pets are for.

My dog Blackie was a Labrador Retriever. He too, was my best friend. He was a beautiful dog. I would play with Blackie for hours at a time. He would chase after us or just follow us around. He was very protective, and would give a warning growl if he thought someone was about to harm us. I think it is good for children to learn the love of animals. It is something that stays with a person throughout their life.

At the end of the block from where I lived, there was a small store. It sold everything from comic books to milk. They also had "penny candy." One of my favorites was a small pack of wax soda pop bottles. The tiny wax bottles came in a box, much like the boxes that hold six of the regular-sized soft drinks. The idea was to bite the wax top off the bottle and drink the liquid inside. The liquid inside wasn't all that great, it was the fact that it came in those neat little wax bottles.

My other favorite was "Buttons." These were small, hard pieces of candy on paper. The paper looked like the long rolls of paper used in an adding machine. There were about 100 pieces of these colored dots on the paper. Of course the store carried soda pop and ice cream bars, which were a big hit with everyone. I can remember turning in pop bottles to get the two cents for the deposit. The store was a magical sort of place for a child. Life seemed so simple then.

It was a time when doctors still made house calls. I remember being sick and our family doctor coming to the house to give me a shot. He then would stop by to see if I was doing better. When someone was sick, the whole neighborhood would know about it, and people would stop in to see how you were doing. The closeness of family and friends would make you feel better.

When I think of my childhood, I remember being happy and having many friends to play with. I was, however, at times, mischievous and had a penchant for exploring the boundaries beyond the realm of good sense. When I was very young, my cousin Tommy and I had the brilliant idea of making a parachute. It seemed simple enough. We would take a pillowcase—climb a ladder to the roof of my uncle's garage—and then jump off. In our pre-jump discussion, the only problem we considered was that we might be carried into the trees as we floated down.

I was to jump first. The leap of faith was more of a fall than a leap. I hit the ground and it knocked the wind out of me. I was lucky that my back and legs were not broken. Tommy did not jump. To this day, I have no desire to jump from the top of a garage roof with just a pillowcase.

I never told my parents about this, as I was sure I would have been punished. In the 1950s there was no such thing as "time out," and in my family there was no "being sent to your room." We were spanked. While I know this practice of discipline has fallen by the wayside, I can honestly say that I deserved every spanking I got. I can also say that it must have been effective, as I never duplicated the bad behavior that would warrant such punishment.

On another occasion, around the age of six, I decided to test the artistic waters. A friend and I decided my next door neighbor's car could use a touch-up. My dad had been painting our house and had left a bucket of paint we thought would be the perfect color. I should also mention that I had on a new coat my mother had bought me for school. We opened the paint bucket and crawled inside the car. We painted the dashboard, the steering wheel, the windshield, and the floorboard.

The next thing I knew was all hell breaking loose. I was "gang-spanked." My neighbor, whose car we had just painted, was actually foaming at the mouth. He was calling me some bad names, but at that moment, verbal insults were not a problem. To this day I have no desire to paint the interior of anyone's car.

The school principal also believed in spanking. There were very few incidents that warranted punishment at school. There was a simple philosophy behind this: Everyone knew that the spanking they got in school would be mild compared to the one they would get from their parents for getting into trouble at school. I am not advocating bringing back paddling in schools. I am just saying that when I went to school, there were few discipline problems.

4

One of the highlights of my childhood was when my Mom got a job at the toy factory. She would bring me all kinds of neat toys. They were all-metal, die-cast toys. Cars, trucks, airplanes, and many military vehicles. I remember Friday as being the day to look forward to a new shiny toy.

Along with my sister Judy, I had my mother and father, Kate and Jessie. They have the traits that I have always tried to cultivate: Hard-working, honest, kind, caring, and thoughtful. I often think what a great world we could have if more people were like my family. When people tell me today that I have made an impact upon their life, I suppose it's just a family tradition.

The neighborhood I grew up in was not the most affluent. It was, in fact, modest surroundings with mostly small Cape Cod-style homes. Many of the homes had but four small rooms. Initially, our house had a hand pump and outside bathroom. I also recall taking baths in a metal tub. My point in telling you this is to point out that I never remember any of these conditions being a hardship. I had loving parents, a great sister, and many friends. A house that is filled with love is the strongest foundation for the positive growth of a child.

I always liked school and was a good student. I was fortunate to have caring and thoughtful teachers. They took pride in the fact that someone was eager to learn, and they made every effort to somehow make each student seem special. I am friends with many teachers today who are great educators. They have the compassion and the desire to see every one of their students excel. The problem is that, in many cases, the teacher has had to become a disciplinarian. Many schools have too many students in the classroom and too many students with behavior problems. A teacher who has to constantly pay attention to a disorderly student cannot give full attention to those students who want to learn.

There were no school shootings, bomb threats, or attacks on teachers. Students had a certain respect for teachers as well as others in positions of authority. It seems to me that schools were successful then because they were more of a learning institution than a correctional facility. Of course, this all stems from the parents. The parents must be actively involved in their child's education. I can recall as a small child, my mother reading books to me, and later, would have me read them to her. Of course this takes time, and many parents today say they "just don't have the time." Time is a valuable commodity. While food, clothing, and shelter are certainly important, the time spent with your children is a necessity that will impact their lives forever.

I was also fortunate to have many good friends as I was growing up. Many of my friends today are those I went to elementary through high school with. As I mentioned earlier, we came from an area that was economically depressed. However, we were all happy because we had nothing to compare it to. The conditions made us closer. We counted on each other and were there for each other. It is important that children have good friends. They learn to share, to relate, and to bond with their friends. On the other hand, a good child (especially an adolescent) can be negatively affected by associating with poor choices of friends. I believe the term "differential association" describes this situation, but I refer to it as "birds of a feather flock together." Some people wonder how a child from a good home and loving parents can turn out to have a negative outlook and direction. Then again, maybe I was just lucky to have the best parents and friends in the world.

I still have many of the same friends today as I had when I was growing up. I went to kindergarten with my friends Jim and Jean Hullinger. I went to junior and senior high school with my good friend Steve Kindell. He is as good a friend today as he was in high school. My friend, Bill Weed and I played baseball together as kids, and eventually started a band together. I played drums, and Bill played guitar. We called ourselves "The Night Riders," and later changed our name to "The Restless Ones." I have been fortunate not only in the number of friends I have, but more importantly, the depth of friendship that we have for one another.

Soon enough my thoughts turned to what most teenage boys' thoughts turn to—girls, cars, and hanging out with my friends. It was also around this age that everyone from my neighborhood went to work. It was understood that we had to work. As I look back on it, it was not so much that we had to work to buy our necessities, but more importantly, our parents knew that work would teach us about responsibility. A child or teenager who is constantly given everything will never learn to value what he or she has. This can also lead to financial irresponsibility later in life.

I started working when I was 13. I had a paper route. It was a paper route that required me to actually sell the newspapers. I would load up a basket on my bike with about 50 newspapers. I would then go into businesses and sell the papers to whoever desired one. I would go into grocery stores, bowling alleys and even taverns. One time, I sold all fifty papers to the same man. He was painting his house and wanted to use the papers as a drop cloth.

Later, when I got my driver's license, I got a job as a cook at a fast-food restaurant. I loved working there because of all the different characters who were employed there. It was a laugh a minute as most of us were teenagers and were easily entertained by the older workers who would be funny just by being who they were.

After a while, I decided that my talents as a french-fry cook would be best served in a more upscale establishment. I then took a job as a chicken cooker at Kentucky Fried Chicken. This was a great job because it paid better than my old job, plus I got free chicken. The highlight of my employment at KFC was to actually meet the Colonel. At that time, Colonel Sanders would come around to inspect his restaurants. I remember the Colonel asking me what particular job I had. I told him I was a cook. He asked me if I had any burns to prove it. It was inevitable that you would get some kind of burn, as the pressure cookers used would sometimes drip hot steam and grease when they were opened. However, I did not know how to respond. I thought I would get in trouble if I replied yes. The store manager was standing behind the Colonel and started nodding his head up and down as if to signal me that it was OK to respond. I then grinned and told the Colonel I had all kinds of burns. He laughed and slapped me on the back. He looked exactly the way he did on the box.

After KFC, I moved on to work at a nursing home. It was a rather religious experience as my job was to baptize dishes. There is something honest about washing dishes, and I actually took pride in my work. I loved this job as I got to interact with all the old people who were residents in the home. There were some real characters there, and I became friends with many of them. Most of them liked us kids who worked there because we would do anything they asked. One gentleman would constantly ask me for crackers. I didn't know that he was on a salt-free diet. I did know he was 101 years old. I suppose I figured anyone who lived to be that old deserved some crackers. One day, the head nurse came into the kitchen and asked if I was passing out crackers to patients. I told her that I had given out a few. She warned me that the crackers could hurt someone and not to do it anymore. Later that week, the nurse searched the old man's room and found 150 packs of crackers! He wasn't eating them. It was like a game to him that he could prove to the nurses he still could get something he wanted. Although I never gave him any more crackers, he would always give me the biggest smile.

After my nursing home experience, I decided that I would like a job with a little more prestige. I got a job selling shoes. "2 pairs/5 dollars," was the slogan of Hills Brothers shoes. I believe it takes a certain type of person to be in sales. Having a good price on the product is half the battle. Once again, it was a valuable experience as I would be meeting and interacting with people from different backgrounds. When I think back on it, these experiences have helped me throughout the years in relating to people.

It was also during this time that I became a volunteer fireman. I had to take all the training of a regular fireman. I carried a portable radio and would respond to fire calls at any time day or night. I was 16 and still in high school. On a few occasions, my monitor would go off during a class, and I would leave the school. I would rush to the firehouse and jump on a truck. We would go put out the fire and return to the firehouse. I was supposed to go back to school, but sometimes I would stick around the firehouse. All the rest of the fireman were older, and they always had colorful stories and jokes to tell. I liked being a fireman and I felt I was doing something good. Something worthwhile. It made me feel good that maybe I was helping someone else.

After Hills Brothers shoes, I took a job with another shoe store. It was an upscale shoe store and it gave me a chance to hone my skills as a salesman. The crowning achievement in my shoe-selling career was when I sold a pair of golf shoes to a man who didn't play golf. They did look nice on him, and he said that he had been thinking about taking up the game.

I remember telling the manager that I was putting in my two weeks' notice. As with all those who employed me, he seemed truly sorry that I was leaving. My next job would be that of a United States Marine.

My adventures began at an early age.

Jessie and Katie Haun.
I was blessed with kind and loving parents.
"An apple doesn't fall too far from the tree."

I think my sister Judy is the best sister in the world. It is no surprise that she became a nurse. She was always caring and compassionate toward others.

   My Mom always kept an eye on my sister and me. She had to. I was *"adventurous."*

My mother was a den mother for Cub Scouts. We participated in an Indian Pow Wow and I begged my dad to give me a Mohawk haircut. It was very hot that day and my head got sunburned. When I went to school the next day, the kids laughed at me so much that I cried and went home.

Chapter 2

"If one dream should fall and break into a thousand pieces, never be afraid to pick one of those pieces up and begin again."

—Unknown

Once a Marine, Always a Marine

"Some people spend an entire lifetime wondering if they made a difference. The Marines don't have that problem."—President Ronald Reagan, 1985

No doubt about it. The Marine Corps defined who I am and what I am about. I still think like a Marine and live my life with the principles I was taught in the Corps. The Marines taught me how to survive, and I have applied that to all aspects of my life.

I joined the Marines in 1970. I was 17 years old, and my parents had to give their permission so I could join. I had signed up on the delayed-entry program. I thought I had 180 days from the date I graduated high school until the time I was to go to boot camp. I was wrong. I had 180 days from the time I signed up. I would be leaving a few weeks after graduating high school. When I think back about it, I wish I could have had a few more weeks.

At the time, the military was not a popular place. The Vietnam War was taking its toll on Marines. The country was split in its attitude about the war, and there were many protests against it. This was a very difficult time in the history of the United States. Personally, I had always wanted to be a Marine. I had, in fact, tried to enlist when I was 15. The recruiter told me to go back to school.

One of the reasons I decided on the Marines was Danny Coleman. He lived in our neighborhood and we went to the same school. He was a few years older than I and would always joke around with my friends and me. I remember the day he came back from boot camp. He was in his uniform and had obviously put on some muscle from the training. You could tell he was proud to be a Marine and he had the usual hard-chargin' talk that all Marines have when they come out of boot camp. "Gary, one Marine is better than 20 Army—better than 50 Air Force—and better than 100 Navy men! They are the best, and there are only two types of people—Marines and those who want to be Marines!"

I didn't get to talk to him much. It was his last day on leave and he was off to Vietnam. Like most of us who grew up in the neighborhood, Danny was very patriotic and proud to be doing his duty. He would write to my sister and tell her about life in the 'Nam.

In one letter he talked about going out on patrols in the jungle and rice paddies. It was his last letter. Danny Coleman was killed in action in 1966 in the Republic of South Vietnam. It seems that war took some of the youngest and the best. Every year I go to the local cemetery where Danny is buried and place an American flag on his grave.

Marine Corps boot camp has always been known as the toughest of all the armed forces. Its basic mission is to turn a civilian into a Marine in 10 weeks. This is accomplished by breaking down the concept of the "individual" and developing an attitude of teamwork. If one individual makes a mistake, everyone else pays for it. Everything is done as a platoon, never individually.

For a Marine entering Recruit Training, the impact of the Corps is immediate. The bus arrives late at night, bringing recruits who have traveled since early morning. Immediately, the DIs (Drill Instructors) are shouting and swarming all over the recruits. The language is salty and peppered with profanity. You have an immediate feeling that the world as you had known it has abruptly ended. This hellish experience proceeds through the night and the recruit undergoes many rapid changes. First, the hair is shaved completely off. Second, all of your civilian clothes are shipped back home. Third, you are issued your military clothing. In a few short hours the individual is already beginning to look like everyone else.

From day one we learned there was only one way to do things— the Marine way. Everything from making your rack (bunk) to shining your boots was done in a specified way. And may God have mercy on your soul if you did not perform a task in the specified way. If your rack was not made properly, the DI would tear it apart and make you do it over and over again. Sometimes, instead of tearing your rack apart, he would have the rest of the platoon tear their bunks apart and remake them. Needless to say, this created some tension between the "un-squared-away" recruit and the rest of the platoon members. This "method of instruction" usually eliminated repetitive mistakes. The strict discipline was applied to all, and this common experience is what brings everyone to think as one.

The training day begins early. After a shower, the platoon is marched to chow. When I was in boot camp, we had metal trays much like those used in prisons. We were given a short time to eat and we developed a habit of eating quickly—a habit I have to this very day.

After chow we would be marched to medical checkups, or to the administrative offices to have ID cards issued, etc. In later weeks this time was spent taking tests. These tests would be used to see what MOS (Military Occupational Specialty) we would be best suited to.

Then would come PT or Physical Training. This might be in the form of running or doing exercises. Usually, the routines would involve push-ups, sit-ups, pull-ups, and a rope climb. There is also a confidence course that has different workout stations. Part of our physical training included close combat self-defense and pugil stick combat. These are sticks with huge pads on each end. They are used to beat your opponent "severely about the head and shoulders." I actually enjoyed this for my first few matches. I was then struck in the ribs and got the wind knocked out of me. I suppose this is what B. F. Skinner was talking about when he used the term "learning by way of negative reinforcement." It must have worked; I started protecting my ribs after that.

During the rest of the day, we would have close order drill and then classes. Close order drill is marching with rifles. The idea was that the platoon made all the correct moves as one. This is an area where the DIs took special pride in the platoon. The DI would often march us in front of another platoon that might be having difficulty with drill movements. He would then stop us and make some disparaging remark about the other platoon being "unmotivated, undedicated," or just being "slime." Of course this led to rivalry with the other platoons; all the while making the individual think less of himself and more of the overall good of the platoon.

Classes consisted of everything from battlefield first aid to instruction on different type of weapons. There were many classes on Marine Corps history. The Marines have quite a history throughout the years. From the Revolutionary War to Desert Storm, the Marines have been "takin' care of business." They have been "the first to fight," and thus the saying—"The Marines have landed, and the situation is well in hand."

One of the most important phases of boot camp is the two weeks spent at the rifle range. Marksmanship is taken very seriously. The first week consists of learning the different firing positions—prone, kneeling, sitting, and offhand (standing). These positions are practiced by "snapping in" or dry firing. The big week, of course, consists of zeroing your weapon and qualification day. When I was in boot camp,

17

we were issued an M-14. In later years I would qualify with an M-16. Qualification day is when all the training comes together. We fired from the 100, the 300, and 500-yard line utilizing the positions named above. From 500 yards a six-foot by six-foot target looks like a postage stamp. The three qualifications are Marksman, Sharpshooter, and Expert. I qualified as a Marksman with the M-14, and later as Expert with the M-16. Personally, the M-16 felt like a BB gun compared to the M-14.

The DIs had a very difficult job. They were responsible for turning a platoon of 75 young men into Marines. There were three drill instructors for every platoon. The senior DI was more like a father figure. He would actually talk to you as a human being. The two other junior DIs were the disciplinarians, and it seemed their job was to make your life a living hell. As a result, we wanted to be the best platoon to avoid the wrath of the DIs.

While learning teamwork, we also learned to get along with one another in a very tough environment. A platoon would include young men from many different backgrounds, different races, different religions, and different economic levels. In their frustration, the drill instructors would quite often use harsh profanity and verbal abuse with the occasional "thumping" or "posture adjustment." Today, DIs are not allowed to use profanity or to physically assault a recruit. I find it interesting that I have heard many young Marines say that they thought boot camp would be tougher and wish it were like it was in the '60s and early '70s. Quite honestly, I feel the Marines of today are just as good as Marines of other time periods. They are well-educated and highly trained. I have talked with many young Marines and would be proud to serve with any of them. They are motivated, dedicated, and proud to be Marines.

The lessons I learned in boot camp are still with me today. I make up my bed every morning, I exercise during the week, and I organize my clothing in a military manner. These habits have served me well, especially as a blind person. Being a Marine is an attitude. An attitude of being competent and confident in yourself. I have carried this attitude with me even after losing my sight. It has strengthened me in dark times. The Marines have a saying— "Adjust, adapt, and overcome," and this is what a blind person must do when facing difficulty or challenges. The Corps taught me not to be afraid of any challenge. I like to think they taught me well.

After boot camp in San Diego, California, it was off to Camp Pendleton for ITR (Infantry Training Regiment). All Marines are trained as combat Marines. This is true of the Commandant, all officers, all enlisted, both men and women. This is one of the things that make the Marines different from the rest of the armed forces. Whether you are a jet mechanic, a unit clerk, a supply officer, or a cook—you are first a "grunt" aka, "groundpounder" or "mud Marine." This philosophy has served the Marine Corps well throughout its history.

ITR is combat training. There are, of course, classes on weapons. At the time I was in, this included all the weapons in the Marine Corps inventory. Weapons included the M-60 machinegun, the LAW (lightweight anti-tank weapon), and the M-79 40 mm grenade launcher. We were also given instruction on the 3.5 rocket launcher (bazooka) and the 106 recoilless rifle. These weapons are no longer in the Marine inventory. As with everything, the Corps now has newer weapons with the latest technology.

We were also introduced to explosives. We were given a quarter stick of dynamite and a military igniter. We would place the igniter into the dynamite, pull the igniter ring, and then we were told to fall into formation. This gets your attention immediately as you do not know how long it takes to ignite the charge. The instructors do. Needless to say, we were marched to safety before the charge went off. We were also taught the correct way to throw a hand grenade and how to set up a Claymore mine. During this course of instruction, we were shown how to set up trip wires and booby traps. The intensity of the training was very serious as many of the Marines would be going to Vietnam after combat training. We all knew some would not be coming back.

As I had scored rather high in my placement tests, I was selected to go to Aviation training. My next destination would be the Naval Air Technical Training Center (NATTC) in Memphis, Tennessee. My first school would be a course on general aviation and safety around aircraft. The next course would be an advanced Mechanical Fundamentals course, which emphasized basic aircraft maintenance. I enjoyed taking all these classes. We had Marine and Navy instructors as well as Navy and Marine students. The instructors were very professional and treated everyone as students. It was so different from the rigid discipline and military etiquette of boot camp.

During this time I was also selected to go into helicopters. Other students would be going into fixed-wing squadrons. I had never really thought about it before, but I had always had a fascination with helicopters. They can hover, fly backwards, and land just about anywhere. They are so versatile. They can be used as gunships, for medical evacuation, as troop and cargo haulers, and so much more. I was happy to be in "helos."

The first part of training was learning the metalsmith trade. Structural Mechanics deals with the structure of the aircraft. All maintenance procedures were taught. Welding, painting, and metal restructuring were a few of the skills that were included in this course. Once again it was a very comprehensive and thorough course of instruction. Everyone paid attention and did their absolute best to pass all the required tests. If a student failed, he would be sent back to advanced infantry training and more than likely to Vietnam. As I said before, some would not be coming back.

During Structural Mechanics school, I was given the opportunity to go into hydraulics. This was a technical field of aviation, as most aircraft rely on hydraulics to control the aircraft. It would mean another six months of training. I was anxious to get out into the Fleet (Fleet Marine Force), but I was told I would pick up the rank of lance corporal if I opted for hydraulics. I found the course interesting, and I was enjoying Memphis. I had started taking karate at a local karate studio and was really getting into it. This was where my interest in the martial arts began.

I was also in the Drum and Bugle Corps in Memphis. There were many advantages to being in this select group. We had a special barracks. It was "laid back" compared to the rest of the barracks on the base. We were also allowed to walk to our classes by ourselves. Everyone else marched in formations. But the best part was the fact that we traveled throughout the South to perform at Marine Corps functions as well as civilian special events. For a young Marine, it was always a pleasure to meet civilians, especially if they were female. I also performed with the Rifle Drill team for a while. I had been in the ROTC drill team in high school and was quite familiar with the movements. We performed in parades and special ceremonies. I really enjoyed this special duty at Memphis, but was happy when my orders came in to go to the Fleet.

20

I arrived at the Marine Corps Air Station (MCAS) New River, North Carolina, in August, 1971. New River was one of the country's largest helicopter bases at the time. It was a beautiful base. Surrounded by tall pine trees, the base was like a helicopter base in the middle of a state park. My new home would be MAG (Marine Air Group) 40. MAG 40 was a training squadron. It was like an on-the-job-training squadron, so Marines who were fresh out of their technical schools could learn by doing. I was eventually assigned to HMHT (Heavy Marine Helicopter) squadron 401. The squadron flew the CH-53 Sikorsky Sea Stallion. It was the largest helicopter in the armed forces inventory. It had two jet engines and six rotor blades. At first glance you would wonder how they managed to fly. But fly they did, and I loved being around them.

MAG 40 was quite the collection of Marines. There were the trainees who were fresh out of their tech schools, and most of the other Marines were just back from Vietnam. The vets from 'Nam were salty, and most were "short timers," meaning they only had a few months left in the Marines. Needless to say, their attitude was laid back and easy-going. The trainees still had that "hard-chargin'—A-Jay-squared-away" attitude. It was quite a mix, but one that worked well. The vets from 'Nam were very professional as they knew their jobs very well and were also very personable. I think they were just happy to know they would be going home soon. It didn't take them long to loosen up the troops. There wasn't as much stress as some of the other Marine units had.

I thought I would be in a training squadron for a couple of months before I went to an operational squadron. However, I was in MAG-40 over a year. The squadron was shorthanded in many areas, and I was needed in my MOS. I really enjoyed MAG 40 and was very happy to serve with them. However, I had a strong desire to get WESPAC (West Pacific) orders. I wanted to go to Vietnam. It probably sounds crazy to say this today, but you have to remember that I was in the Marine Corps—and their mission is to "take care of business." Many years have now passed, and after my time in the veterans hospital, I now know that Vietnam was not the great crusade. It saddens me to think of the young men who lost their lives in that war. It also saddens me that the men and women who went to 'Nam were never really accepted into society after the war. Many people don't seem to understand that when you are in the military, you go where they say they want you to go. There are no choices, there is no negotiation, and there is no option. I only hope that when you read this it will give you some deeper thoughts on Memorial Day and Veterans Day.

During my time with MAG40, I was cross training in more than one MOS. In other words, I was doing different jobs. I would also be sent to different bases for additional schools and training. One of my favorites was Cherry Point, North Carolina—home of the 2nd Marine Air Wing. Cherry Point was where many of my advanced hydraulics schools were located. There was a NARF (Naval Air Rework Facility) there, and it was an opportunity to work with civilian instructors. In my particular case, my instructors were some of the nicest people I have ever met. There were no Marine regulations, and the training was excellent.

It was also during this time that I was selected to fly on many of the squadron's cross-country flights. HMHT-401 not only was a training squadron for enlisted personnel, but for pilots as well. Some of the pilots were fresh from Naval Aviation school, while others were seasoned pilots who were transitioning from one type of helicopter to another. In some outfits in the Marines, there is sometimes tension between the officers and enlisted men. I rarely found this to be the case during my time with Marine Aviation. I think it had something to do with the fact that the pilots understood you were responsible for the maintenance of the aircraft they were flying in. The relationship between pilots and air crewmen has always been close.

Many of our pilots needed cross-country flying experience. It just so happened that one of the flights went to Knoxville, Tennessee. As I had many relatives in that area, I made sure I would be on that flight. It was nice, as I would have an uncle or aunt pick me up at the airport and return me when we were scheduled to go back to New River. It was on one of these visits that my aunt introduced me to a young lady who lived down the street from her. Her name was Donna Packard. Donna lived with her father who was 86 at the time. She was adopted, and her mother had died in a car accident when she was very young. Donna was still in high school and quite shy. She was the nicest person I have ever met. She was charming in that sweet, Southern way. I suppose you could say it was love at first sight. She would tell me later that when she first saw me in my dress blues, that she never forgot that day. She said it was the happiest day of her life. I started making all the cross-country flights to Tennessee.

In mid-1972 I was assigned to an operational squadron. MAG 40 was being decommissioned. My new home would be HML (Helicopter Marine Light) 268. It was a brand new squadron and I would be helping to start it up and get it going. I remember this as one of the happiest times in my life. I had been promoted to meritorious corporal in MAG 40 and was now doing the job of a staff sergeant. The Marines are good at giving a NCO (Non-Commissioned Officer) a lot of responsibility, thus the term, "NCOs are the backbone of the Marine Corps." I had my own office, plus I had several people working for me; and was considered one of the squadron's top NCOs. I was 20 years old.

HML 268 flew the UH-1E (known as Hueys) and the UH-1N. These were very versatile aircraft, and our flight schedule would vary from day to day. Sometimes we would be assigned VIP flights to carry high-ranking officers from place to place. The next day we would be conducting aerial gunnery training. We might be assigned to assist the Search and Rescue unit at Cherry Point or Combined Exercise training with Army Green Berets. And of course we also had our cross-country flights, with me making sure I was on every flight to Tennessee. Donna and I were becoming very close, and we would write love letters to each other. We couldn't wait to see each other. She even talked her Dad into coming to New River to visit me. I took her to the ocean and we walked along the beach. It is nice to be young and in love.

On July 14th, 1973, I was asked to help out the Headquarters and Maintenance squadron, as they needed some hydraulic power to check out a landing gear unit. I had done this hundreds of times. A person has to be qualified to run certain pieces of ground support gear. With all my schools, I was checked out on and had a license to run, an NC-8 (an electric generator truck used to start aircraft), TA-75 (an aircraft towing vehicle), CCC (corrosion control cart used to pressure-wash the aircraft, especially after we had been out over the ocean or doing carrier qualifications), MS1 High Air Compressor (used mostly to inflate the tires of aircraft), and the HT-64 (a hydraulic test stand used to power the hydraulics of an aircraft while it is on the ground).

I made all the connections and began to apply the power. The test stand had a throttle that was pushed to increase power. The unit could produce up to 3,000 pounds psi (per square inch) of power. I throttled it up and felt a slight vibration in the front of the unit. I walked around to check it out and was standing over the hose that connected the stand to the aircraft.

In a split second, I noticed the hose leaking; and in another split second, the hose came loose. In another split second, I was down and momentarily unconscious. The hose had literally exploded in my face. The hose hit me on the side of the neck and also flooded my eyes with hydraulic fluid that was under high pressure.

Although I was bleeding (surprisingly, through my nose) my pain was focused in my eyes. It was as if my eyes had been pushed into the back of my head. In the ambulance on the way to the hospital, I tried to open my eyes. I couldn't. The Navy corpsman had me open them so he could flush them out. This procedure was done again at the New River Hospital Facility. When I was able to open my eyes, they burned a little but there was no severe pain. It seemed like hours at the New River Hospital before I was transferred to Camp Lejeune Naval Hospital. I was scared to death. When I opened my eyes, I couldn't see.

I was at the Naval Hospital for several days. The doctors first diagnosed my problem as retinal trauma. The Navy doctors were very good about talking to me honestly and openly. An eye specialist was brought in and told me that I had retina inflammation. He said he wanted some other eye specialists to look at my eyes. He also told me he was in contact with Bethesda Naval Hospital. He said he either wanted to have me transported up there or to have one of their top specialists come to see me. All through this time, I was just hoping for my sight to come back. It is a sickening feeling. I felt helpless and I was going crazy about the situation I was in.

One morning I opened my eyes and could see something. It wasn't much, but at the time I thought it was a miracle. I thought my eyes were getting better. I was able to tell if the lights were on or off. However, the next day it was like it was before. I was depressed, worried, dejected, scared, and all the while hoping to get my eyesight back. When the eye doctor returned, he said I was now permanently blind in both eyes and that there was no operation or cure for my eyes.

I felt his words rip through me, and again had a multitude of emotions—none of them good.

For the next few weeks, I had several sessions with counselors. They told me that I would have to learn to re-adjust. I was advised of the rehabilitation programs that were available. I was hoping I would wake up one day and everything would be all right. I wanted to stay in the Marine Corps and make a career out of it. I was mostly frustrated and depressed. Some things in life are hard to explain.

My retirement orders were read to me by a Marine officer. They stated that I was to be permanently retired by reason of physical disability. I was issued a Grey (Military Retiree's ID) and told my retirement certificate would be mailed to me. I had always dreamed of retiring from the Marine Corps. I knew I would have stayed in 20 or maybe 30 years. I was still hoping that one day I could have an operation and maybe go back in the Corps. It has been 27 years now, and I am still hoping.

    I joined the Marine Corps at age 17. With the exception of the birth of my son, the proudest moment in my life was when I earned the right to wear the eagle, globe and anchor, and the title of Marine.

All Marines are basic riflemen and must learn combat skills. From the Commandant down to the newest recruit, all are taught marksmanship and small unit tactics. This picture was taken in 1970, at Camp Pendleton, California, while I was in ITR (Infantry Training Regiment).

Chapter 3

"We cannot change yesterday. We can only make the most of today, and look with hope toward tomorrow."

Someone to Light the Path

During my stay at the hospital, I had called Donna and told her what was going on. She was very reassuring, and told me that no matter what, she loved me. This was like an anchor that kept me from spinning out of control with self pity and despair. In one of our conversations, she told me that I was welcome to stay with her and her father in their home in Tennessee. Until this time, I always figured I would go back to my hometown of Rockford, Illinois. The more I talked to Donna, the more I knew I would be going to Tennessee.

When Donna and her dad came to pick me up, I thought it might be an awkward moment. It was quite the opposite. We were so happy to be with one another. When we got back to their home in Tennessee, they had a room all ready for me.

Donna's dad had a home located near Oak Ridge, Tennessee. Oak Ridge is also called "The Atomic City," as it was part of the Manhattan Project in World War II. The uranium enrichment plant made the ingredients for the atomic bomb. There is quite a history connected with the city. To this day, the city still has a large number of scientists and several top-secret research projects going on.

Donna's dad, Mr. Jack Packard, was an elderly gentleman. His driver's license showed he had been born in 1889. He'd had many experiences over his lifetime and would sit for hours talking about the "days gone by." He was a retired electrician from the uranium enrichment plant. One of his favorite stories was how he lost his right index finger to a bolt of electricity. For a man of advanced years, he got around pretty well. He still drove, and smoked cheap cigars. He was a good and honest man, and loved animals. At the time of my arrival, he had 11 dogs and six cats. He would feed them three times a day, and the animals would follow him around.

Mr. Packard's house was located in an area known as Marlow. He had seven acres and a house that was quite old but quite comfortable. Across the street were a country church and an elementary school. Down the street was an honest-to-goodness general store where you could purchase anything from water pipe to coloring books. The people in Marlow were friendly and down-to-earth. It was a blend of Southern hospitality and back-hills insights on life. The peaceful, sleepy atmosphere was only shaken by the 100-car trains that would pass by. After a while though, the trains seemed to somehow fit in, and they became part of this country postcard.

Donna and I became very close in a short period of time. We needed each other. We completed each other, and we were everything the other needed or wanted. My being blind was not an issue as "love conquers all." We made each other stronger, and I didn't feel disabled around Donna. I could have gone to rehabilitation and counseling at this time, but felt like I had a sense of belonging, a sense of purpose, and a sense of positive direction. This was due to the constant attention from Donna. To others, she would appear to be shy and quiet. However, when I think about those early days and remember the laughter and fun we had, I know she had a positive energy that illuminated the paths of others.

One day we decided to go to a fair in Knoxville. We rode all the rides and sat under shade trees and just talked. It was getting near evening and we decided to just sit down on the grass and relax. Donna told me that I was the greatest thing that had ever happened to her, and that she was so happy just to be near me. I told her I felt the same way about her. We kissed one of those kisses that are shared by two young people who are in love. I asked her to marry me.

We were married on September 1st, 1973. It was a storybook moment. We walked across the street to the small church. The minister for the church was just a young man himself, and we were the first couple he had ever performed a wedding ceremony for. He was very nervous, but was so nice and caring. I was in my dress blues and had two of my friends from the Marines as best men. Donna was absolutely beautiful in her wedding dress. It was a simple, yet very touching ceremony. It was one of life's most beautiful moments. It was like something you would see in a movie.

We went to Pigeon Forge for our honeymoon. We were so much in love and just wanted to be close to one another. Donna told me she was the happiest person in the world. I felt the same. We knew we were good for each other. We were as "one," and we made each other better people.

I remember the first years of marriage as being filled with happiness. We would travel to see my relatives who lived in nearby cities, and on the weekend go to the public swimming pool. It was also at this time that I got back into karate. Donna also took lessons.

Donna loved animals, and we would go to the local farmers market where cows, horses, goats, chickens, and all other types of livestock were sold. On one of these trips, Donna saw a horse she described as "the most beautiful horse in the world." Although I knew absolutely nothing about horses, I started negotiating a price for the horse. I knew Donna wanted the horse, and that was good enough for me. I bought her the horse and a new saddle. She was so happy she cried.

In 1975, our son William (Billy) Joseph was born. He was born at the University of Tennessee Hospital in Knoxville. He was 8 lbs. 11 oz., and 21 inches in length. The doctor had me put on a hospital mask and gown because he wanted me to actually help in the delivery room. As soon as Billy was born, I got to touch him and he held on to my fingers. The doctor said, "You have a beautiful son, Gary." It was the greatest moment of my life. There is no way to describe this feeling. I suppose you have to go through the experience to know.

Donna and I were so happy during this time. Billy was everything to us. He was a very good baby. He always seemed to be happy, and was a joy to hold and feed. As he grew older, he was always playful and loved the attention that he got from his mother and me. We would sit on the floor and play with him for hours. He learned to walk at about 2, and was talking baby talk at about the same time. One of the most precious things I have is a tape recording of Billy saying his A-B-Cs and later singing songs that he liked.

It was about this time that I knew I had to get into a serious rehabilitation program. The state of Tennessee had done some things for me, but I knew that the program at Hines Veterans Hospital was the best in the world. I also wanted Billy to attend school in my hometown of Rockford, Illinois. At the time, some of the schools in the area were not that good. Donna did not have a very good education and had trouble reading and writing. She wanted Billy to have the best education we could possibly give him. She agreed that the move to Illinois would be the best thing for him.

We moved to Rockford in 1977. I entered the Basic Blind Rehabilitation Program at Hines Veterans Hospital as soon as we moved. I have a chapter about my training later in this book. I was in the program for 16 weeks, and I would come back to Rockford to see Donna and Billy on the weekends. After I learned to use the cane, I would take the bus home on Friday and return to the hospital on Sunday night.

We bought a home that was across the street from where my parents lived. It happened to be across the street from the house I grew up in as a child. It was a small but comfortable home. Billy was growing older and had many friends to play with. His favorite time of year was Halloween. He liked the different costumes, and we would decorate the house for him. One year we turned our garage into a "haunted house," and let the neighborhood kids go through it. We hired a few high school students to pose as witches, ghosts, and other characters. It was quite a production.

I had been introduced to magic while I was in the hospital, and began classes at a local magic shop. I also began karate lessons again. I talk more about these endeavors later in the book. However, our lives were good, and Donna and I grew stronger by the day. We then decided to bring Donna's dad up to Illinois to live with us. He was in his 90s, and was beginning to have some problems getting around. It made Donna very happy to have her dad living with us.

In 1978 I began competing in karate tournaments again. It was also about this time that Donna became interested in running, and joined the YMCA to work out and to make use of their running path. She was a natural at running and was very fast. It wasn't long before she started competing in 10k foot races and other events. She almost always won something for running and liked to compete. She was injury prone, but would always come back stronger.

In 1978 Donna and I went to a magicians convention in Las Vegas. Donna was a great magician's assistant, and liked the excitement of doing a magic show. We would do stage illusions such as the sword box and the zigzag lady, where Donna's petite figure was an advantage. She would be "cut in half and stabbed with eight swords," and then be restored at the end of the routine. We had a great time in Vegas and met with many of the world's greatest magicians.

Donna loved animals and actually encouraged me to start working with doves and rabbits. She would treat the animals as pets. In fact, she fed one of the rabbits so well that we could not use him in the show anymore. He had become a big, furry critter much like a soft beanbag chair. Although we couldn't use him in the show, Donna would bring him out at the end so the children could pet this "cotton ball blimp." She was equally loving to the doves I used and would give them showers with a spray bottle.

In 1980 we went to a magic convention in Hawaii. Donna was thrilled to be going and bought a brand new camera for the trip. Once again the top magicians in the world were at the convention. Donna and I also went to the Pearl Harbor Memorial, the Punch Bowl military cemetery, Chinatown, and of course we spent a lot of time on Waikiki Beach. Donna told me on the way back home that I was the "real magic" in her life. She said she often thought about how I had come into her life, and that she was so very happy.

In 1981 we moved to our new home. We had come quite a way since our first year of marriage. From Mr. Packard's house, to our house trailer, to our small home in my old neighborhood. We now had moved into a bi-level on the end of a cul-de-sac. It was, and still is, a very pleasant neighborhood. Donna began furnishing the house with furniture that would turn the house into a home.

That summer we began a process of planting many different shrubs, ferns, and flowers around the house. Today, the house is surrounded by flower gardens and evergreens. The tree that stands by my mailbox was only a small stick growing out of the ground. Most of the trees in the neighborhood were much the same. They are a tribute to time. They have seen many families come and go in the neighborhood. They have weathered many harsh winters and storms. Every fall they turn into brilliant colors, and then the explosion of color gives way to the winter tree. It all begins again in spring. I suppose it is much like the growth of a person. A tree is born by way of a seed and grows through the sprouting process. It seems every year they are reborn and begin anew.

During this time Billy began school. It was one of our greatest pleasures to watch him grow and to learn. He was making friends at school and in the neighborhood. The school he attended was very progressive and encouraged the students to express themselves in many different ways. I personally think this was the foundation for his talent in art. He was quite expressive even at an early age.

Donna's dad lived with us until his health failed. He became unmanageable, and we decided that he might do better in a nursing home. It was a good decision, as he actually got better both physically and mentally during his stay. In fact he got better to the point we brought him back to live with us. He lived with us many months thereafter. He would sit and watch TV until he would fall asleep.

Then, one fall afternoon, with the sun shining on his face, he fell asleep for the final time.

I was downstairs and Donna came to me and said, "I think Dad died." I told her to sit down, and I went up to his room. I checked his pulse on the side of the neck and knew he had died. I called the fire department and they responded right away. They tried the usual methods to revive him, but it was not to be. They took him to the hospital, and after a while a doctor came out and told us that his heart had just stopped. He was 96 years old. He was a good man and loved animals. I can only hope that people will say that about me when it is my time to go.

I suppose running and bicycling were Donna's way to deal with her father's passing. She would run seven days a week and on many days, go for a 50-mile bike ride after she ran. When I would tell her that she should slow down a little, she would become angry. I knew she needed time to deal with the loss of her father, but I was concerned about her health and well-being. Over the next few years, Donna would compete in several more 10k foot races as well as marathons and triathlons. Her biking events included a few 24-hour bike races.

By 1990 Billy was in high school and doing quite well. He was on the wrestling team, and we went to many of his events. He was a good kid and Donna and I were very proud of him. It made us happy to see him doing well in school. In junior high he was in the Creative and Performing Arts program, and once again I feel this strengthened his talent and interests in art.

It was around 1991 that Donna began making some new "friends." I was always supportive of Donna in everything she attempted or any endeavor she would get involved in. However, as she began doing more and more things with her "friends," she began spending less and less time at home. When I think back on this, I wish I had reacted in a strong way. I didn't. I wanted Donna to be happy.

In 1992 we took Billy on a Caribbean cruise. It was with Royal Caribbean and was on the "Sovereign of the Seas," at that time one of the largest cruise boats in service. It was like a floating palace. The food was the best I have ever had, and there was entertainment nightly. The ship would stop at different islands and we would go shopping and then relax on the beautiful beaches. Billy and I would swim in the ocean or just float around on the giant floats that the ship provided. It was a great time and Donna and I had planned another cruise for the following year. It would be our 20th anniversary.

The following year Donna began spending more and more time away from home. She was also acting strangely at times. While she had just hired an interior decorator to remodel our home, she also wanted to move into a bigger home. This was unusual, as she had always talked of moving into a more manageable home after Billy moved away. She would also become very agitated if I mentioned anything about her slowing down on her activities. On September 1st, 1993, we celebrated our 20th wedding anniversary.

In 1994 Donna's behavior became erratic. When I would ask her to drive me somewhere, she would always have to be doing something for somebody else. She would go over to her friends' house and cook them meals, but would bring me fast food. I never complained about this as it became a way of life, and I figured it was just a stage of life that she was going through. She would only get three or four hours of sleep at night, but would go ballistic when I told her she needed to rest. Still, I thought this would pass in time. Once I insisted that she go to a doctor and she exploded with anger.

On an early fall morning, I received a call from Donna. She was at a lawyer's office and she said she wanted a divorce. I couldn't believe it. At the time I was in a state of shock, and I told her we would talk about it when she got home. When she came home, it was like talking to someone I had never met in my life. She was a different person. I was devastated. I pleaded with her not to go through with this. I literally begged her to reconsider. I didn't know why she would do this. I now know she really didn't know why either.

The first two weeks after Donna left were some of the darkest days in my life. When I talk to people about walking in the valley, I know what I'm talking about, because I've been there. It was a hellish experience. I know what depression is because I was at the lowest point a person can go. It was not a matter of feeling lonely. It was a matter of feeling helpless. I didn't feel bad because I was blind and going through this. I just felt bad that Billy had to go through it. And just as importantly, I knew Donna was heading down a path of self-destruction. It was as if she was in a tailspin and could not pull out.

I don't think it would serve any purpose to talk about how Donna treated me at this time. She had turned into a person I didn't know, and she was burning bridges behind her. After a period of time, I got tired of going from room to room and crying. I knew I had to get it together and proceed with my life. I wanted to be a good father to Billy, and knew I couldn't do that if I was sad all the time. I felt as if I had been knocked down, but was now able to stand up and get back into the game of life. I was putting it all into perspective. I would go on with my life. The divorce was over with and I became philosophical about it. If that is what Donna wanted to make her happy, then so be it. Then I got a visit from Donna.

I was downstairs typing a letter. She had come through the front door, and I heard someone coming down the stairs. I thought it was Billy and said, "Son, is that you?" "No, it's me." Donna was standing right behind me. I literally jumped out of the chair. Before I could say anything, she said she just wanted to talk to me. She tried to hug me and I felt a folded up newspaper in her hand. When I asked her what that was, she said she had a newspaper clipping to give to Billy. She was talking very softly as if she was sleepy or drowsy. I was scared and told her I was going to call the police. She followed me upstairs, and as I was reaching for the phone she hugged me tightly and said, "Gary, I will always love you. The divorce was the biggest mistake of my life, and I am so sorry for what I have done to you. It haunts me the way I treated you." I was still in shock, and told her that she needed help and that she should talk to her friends. She told me she didn't have any friends. I told her that I was her friend and that we were best friends for years. She then said she knew that and that was why she was going to kill herself. Before I could say anything she said, "Take care of Billy. I love him and I love you too." She then ran out to her car and drove off.

I called the police to file a report, and they said they would investigate. I called her friends to let them know that if she came to talk to them, that she needed help. I would find out later that she had gotten a gun from a guy she had been with. No one heard from Donna for about four days. On that fourth day at about 5 o'clock in the evening, there was a knock on my door. When I answered it, a man said, "Mister Haun, I'm the chaplain for the Rockford Police Department."

I immediately started crying uncontrollably. The chaplain came in and was speaking, but I was going to pieces. Then I ran in to tell Billy. I could hardly talk. It was a nightmare. The police chaplain then told me the details of how they had found Donna. I cannot describe to you how I felt. I can only say it is the worst feeling in the world. I cried and I cried. It is very difficult to write about this. I loved Donna very much, and I know in her right mind that she would have never done anything to hurt Billy or me.

I cried for days, all day long. I went over to the house that she had just bought and picked out the clothes for her funeral. I made the arrangements and tried to be strong for Billy. I wasn't. I cried throughout the funeral and was probably on the verge of a nervous breakdown. Billy was my strength to get on with my life.

There are many things in this life we do not understand. I suppose it is better to have loved someone deeply than to never know the feeling of being in love. We are born, and some day we will die. Someone who takes their own life deprives themselves of the joy of life. I know they do not truly know what they are doing. To them it is the only way they can deal with their situation. If you or anybody you know ever talks of suicide, please seek help. There are people who can help you. Don't be afraid to reach out and ask for help.

I choose not to remember the bad times during the last days of Donna's life. No, I choose to remember the good times we had. The early days when we met, the feeling of the two of us as one person, the sweet, down-to-earth person she was, and the happiness we shared in watching Billy grow to become a fine young man. I remember her kindness and thoughtfulness. The Native Americans believed that a person never really dies as long as that person lives on in the memories of others. I think this is so.

The happiest day of our lives was when our son, Billy, was born. We loved to take him to new places. He was an exceptionally good baby and was always smiling.

Donna loved doing the magic shows. We performed for schools, companies, festivals, and several conventions.

In 1992 we went on a Caribbean cruise. We had a great time and participated in all the ship's activities, which included a talent show and a costume party. We won 1st place in both.

Chapter 4

"The harder the conflict, the more glorious the triumph. What we obtain too cheap, we esteem too lightly; it is dearness only that gives everything its value. I love the man that can smile in trouble, that can gather strength from distress and grow brave by reflection."

"Tis the business of little minds to shrink; but he whose heart is firm, and whose conscience approves his conduct, will pursue his principles unto death."

—*Thomas Paine*

Reflections from Yesterday, View for Tomorrow

"What about an eye transplant?" "Why don't you have an operation?" "I know a doctor who can remove cataracts, I bet he could help you."

I probably have been asked these questions a thousand times. I appreciate the concern that initiates these inquiries. However, if any of these procedures would help, I would have had them many years ago. The human eye is very complicated in the way it works.

An eye transplant is essentially to replace the lens or cornea on the front part of the eye. My problem is on the retina, on the back of the eye. Thus, in my case, an eye transplant would be like changing the lens on a camera that has no film in it.

When I first lost my sight, everything looked hazy and blurry. It was much like looking through welder's goggles that had been smeared with grease. I thought this would eventually get better. It didn't. In fact, like a thief in the night, it seemed with each day, the welder's goggles got darker and the grease got heavier. I would also get bright flashes of light, even in a completely dark room. This light would be like someone flashing a camera within inches of my eye.

I still thought that after time, my sight would come back. However, a Navy doctor explained that my condition was permanent, and that my prognosis was not good. He explained that there was no cure or operation that would restore my sight. Like many things in life, some things are hard to understand. Why me? Why now? I was 21 years old and a sergeant in the Marine Corps. Although I talked to many counselors, it was my CO (Commanding Officer) who got me thinking on the right track. "Sgt. Haun, you're the same person you always were. You will just have to learn to do some things differently."

Like many people, I had many misconceptions about blindness and blind people. And, like many newly blinded people, I did not want to be "blind." I wanted to be "normal." I tried to act "normal" by bluffing sight that I did not have. I did not want people feeling sorry for me or treating me as if I were "abnormal." I would try to get around without using a cane. However, after many bumps, bruises, and cuts, I knew I would have to change my perspective. I then became a normal blind person. And, just as my CO said, I am the same person I always was, and now I just do things in a different way.

Today I often hear people say, "Gary, I almost forget that you're blind." The fact is, they see the normality. I may have Braille dots on my microwave, but I can do my own cooking. I may have raised marks on my washing machine, but I do my own laundry. I make my bed every morning, just as I did in the Corps. I may use a talking calculator, but I balance my own checkbook. I…well, you get the picture. It's not so much what I do differently, it's that I just do.

Chapter 5

"One of the most tragic things I know about human nature is that all of us tend to put off living. We are all dreaming of some magical rose garden over the horizon—instead of enjoying the roses that are blooming outside our windows today."

—Dale Carnegie

Vision and a Vision

Many people have asked me if there is any positive thing about being blind. Most are referring to the idea that if you lose one sense, other senses become stronger. Let me be perfectly honest. I do not like being blind, and it can at times make life rather difficult. However, I try not to let it control my life. I also try not to let it limit me from leading a positive life. Also, my other senses are the same as any other person has; it's just that I have to rely on my other senses more than others do. Thus, it would appear that my hearing and sense of touch is extraordinary.

I have found that in working with children who are born blind (congenitally blind), learn to do things as a blind person. The negative side is that concept recognition can be very difficult. However, as in my case, losing one's eyesight later in life (adventitiously blind), can have its positive and negative. On the positive side, concept recognition is not as difficult. What is difficult is the adjustment and frustration that can take place as a result of having to learn a different way of doing things.

As with most things in life, attitude is very important whether blind or sighted. When I first went to the Blind Rehabilitation Center at Hines Veterans Hospital, I realized something that would change my life. I noticed that some of the people in the hospital were very negative about their situation; they seemed to be very dependent on others, and were pessimistic about their futures. The other half were quite the opposite.

They were as positive as possible under the circumstances, wanted to learn to be independent, and tried to be optimistic that their lives would be productive and as normal as any other person's.

It was then and there that I made a conscious decision on how I wanted to live my life. It was my choice. It was not my choice to become blind, but it was my choice on how I would live my life as a blind person. I would try to do my best, and while I was at it, keep a positive attitude. And that is that.

Just as the Marine Corps gave me the physical and mental skills to adapt and overcome, Hines Veterans Hospital Blind Center would give me the skills and techniques to adapt and overcome blindness.

Hines is the pioneer in blind rehabilitation. Their program began many years ago, and really became organized when training many of the blinded veterans from World War II. Over the years they have became the "state of the art" program in blind rehabilitation. It is the highest quality instruction available.

All of the staff are highly trained professionals who not only teach techniques, but help in restoring self-confidence, self-esteem, and a positive self-image. I like to think of Hines as the Marine Corps of blind rehabilitation. And I think that is just about the best compliment any organization can have.

The Basic Course at Hines is a sixteen-week program, and covers many different skills such as Braille, orientation and mobility, living skills, communication skills, manual skills, and recreation skills. For the advanced graduate, electronic aids and appliances and computer training may be offered. All these subjects are covered with the idea of improving the veteran's confidence. Counseling is also provided, with sessions with the staff psychologist as well as group therapy.

Basic Braille is like learning the ABCs all over again. Basically, Braille is made up of a cell of six dots. Different formations of the dots make up the alphabet. Grade One Braille is essentially the alphabet, numbers, and some punctuation marks. Grade Two Braille is made up of contractions. I suppose the best way to describe contractions that it's a lot like shorthand. A certain Braille dot can represent an entire word.

I was also introduced to Grade Three Braille, which is like super shorthand. I was taught this as I would be attending college after I left the Blind Center, and this can be used for note taking. It is easy to understand that advanced Braille can be a real time saver over using Grade One and having to write every word letter by letter.

To be perfectly honest, my Braille skills are not as sharp as they used to be. This is because I rarely read Braille books. I usually read my books by listening to "talking books" or books on cassette tape. I also have a reading machine which I use to read most other printed matter. I use Braille mostly for marking items such as cassette tapes, CDs, prescription medicine bottles, and other everyday items. I also use Braille to label settings on my microwave oven, washing machine, and other appliances that I need to know where the setting is.

Orientation and Mobility (O and M) is the science of cane travel. These skills have been perfected over many years since the days of the wooden white cane. As a matter of fact, I was taught to use the aluminum prescription cane when I was going through the basic course. When I returned recently, I was given the new graphite cane, which is lighter and gives back better tactile information than the older type of cane. I was amazed at the difference in the feel of the two canes. The new cane is like the "stealth fighter" of canes.

Before cane travel is introduced, the blind person is taught to move around safely without a cane. This is done by holding one arm across the face and the other arm diagonally below the waist. I use this technique daily, and it has saved me from many bumps and bruises. Also, the blind person is shown the technique of using a sighted guide. This is done by holding on to a sighted person's arm, just above the elbow. This transmits such information to the blind person as which direction the person is going and when to stop. This is also the best technique for following someone through a crowded area, as it is easy to tell which way the person is turning.

Cane travel is introduced in stages. First, you must learn to use the cane properly. The technique is to arc the cane as you step forward, much as if you were kicking the cane to sweep the area ahead of you. I am amazed that many people think blind people just "poke and hope" with a cane. However, they do appreciate a good cane traveler even though they do not know the science behind it.

Cane travel progresses from getting around the blind center to getting around the main hospital. This is also good for helping with memory cues. It is important to listen for things such as elevator bells, automatic doors, and high traffic volume areas such as entrance doors and hallways. Also, the subtle rise or decline of a surface is a good cue. Some hallways, such as the one leading to the blind center, have a distinct echo.

The next progression is outside the hospital and into the surrounding community. This means memorizing streets and landmarks. It is also a time when traffic crossings become part of the experience. You are taught to listen to the flow of traffic and to cross traffic in a very methodical manner. I must admit I am still sometimes apprehensive about crossing traffic. When I went to the hospital for computer training, I requested a refresher O and M class and it helped me greatly in terms of confidence in my travel skills.

In the advanced stages of O and M, the veteran learns to catch a bus, ride the subway, go shopping, and generally how to deal with many different mobility situations. This is done by traveling in different areas such as rural areas, mall settings, and urban settings. On my final O and M lesson, I had to catch a bus at the hospital, go to the subway station, catch a train, and go to downtown Chicago. This is quite a confidence builder because you realize that if you can do this, you can travel just about anywhere you want to go.

As you gain mobility skills, you also gain independence. You no longer have to depend on someone else to take you somewhere. Independence is important. Being confident enough with your travel skills to go into a new situation is a great feeling.

I feel I should mention something about guide dogs. Just about everyone I've ever met has asked me why I don't have a guide dog. While dogs are good for some blind people, they are not for all blind people. Someone who is good with cane travel might not want nor need a dog. There probably is an extra degree of safety in having a dog, as they can see danger areas and can keep you away from them. A dog can also be a great companion and a best friend. Personally, I love dogs, and some day will go and take the necessary training to get a guide dog. However, I am comfortable with my travel skills and almost always travel with a friend. I have many friends who have guide dogs, and it certainly is a thing of beauty, the chemistry between the two. I don't think there is any greater bond that a person has for an animal, than an animal that is depended upon so much. A guide dog is truly an angel with four legs.

In Living Skills the veteran is taught to do those daily skills that are so important for day-to-day living. This can sometimes be frustrating because you must relearn how to do things that once were easy and took no time at all. However, the staff understands this, and in a very professional way teaches you how to master these skills. Cooking, housecleaning, and laundry are but a few of the areas taught in living skills. Methods of marking with raised dots on appliances and organizing items in a methodical way are part of these skills. I can remember the feeling of independence when I could, by myself, do my own laundry and cooking. To this day, I still clean my house, do my laundry, and cook my food. While this may seem rather ordinary to most people, I take pride in doing these everyday tasks. I use the training I received in Living Skills on a daily basis, and it certainly is a path to independence.

Communication Skills include such things as using letter guides to write out letters in longhand. This is accomplished by using a plastic template that has windows that keep your writing straight. There are also guides for envelopes, checks, cassettes, etc. Also, you learn to type. The only difference in the typewriter is that there are tactile dots on the letters F and J, so it is easier to find the home row. I also have the dots on the numbers 1, 5, and 0. My computer keyboard is set up the same way. I was also taught to type while listening to a tape recorder. This skill is very handy as I often record information that I will later type up.

My Manual Skills training was actually in two different classes. First I was introduced to leather working. The importance of this is relearning manual dexterity without the use of your eyes. Many of the skills in everyday life require good manual dexterity. I also remember Manual Skills training as a time to learn to relax. You must remember that the Blind Center course is much like going to school. I would begin the day with one hour of Orientation and Mobility. Then I would have an hour of Braille. I would then go to Living Skills for another hour. And so it went for eight hours—each class was like learning a different subject.

In Advanced Manual Skills, I was taught woodworking and basic household maintenance. I would turn wood on a lathe to make a lamp, or use a sander to smooth down a board for a footstool. Once again I really enjoyed this, and I gained confidence around power tools. Tim the Tool Man would be proud. The training I received in basic home maintenance has also served me well. Everything from replacing sink washers to repairing holes in the wall was covered. There is a great feeling of accomplishment in being able to do something yourself. I like the word able better than disable.

All during the training program, the veteran is introduced to different Recreation Skills. This is, in fact, where I first played a game of golf. Essentially, someone lines me up on the tee and in the fairway. I attempt to advance the ball toward the green (after all, this is the objective). Once on the green, someone walks me across the green so I can get an idea of the line I have to take. I also have someone tap on the pin as it helps me define where the cup is. I must admit that I am not a very good golfer, however, there are many good blind golfers.

Near the end of training, the veteran is introduced to the many electronic aids and appliances. These range anywhere from the Laser Cane to the Sonic Guide. These are items that send out a signal and return it to the blind person as either an audible signal or a tactile stimulation. They help in mobility. Technology is a wonderful thing, and it only gets better and better. Synthesized speech has come a long way since I was first introduced to it. At first it was very robotic, and one had to have a keen ear to decipher it. Now it is very human-like and very understandable. Progress in synthesized speech has been great for the visually impaired. There are now talking watches, calculators, clocks, and of course, computers.

If the Basic Rehabilitation course can be compared to going to elementary and high school, then Advanced Computer training is like going to college. Advanced Computer Technology is offered to certain veterans as part of a graduate program. Personally, I do not know how I managed without my computer. In fact, I am writing this book using it.

As I type, the computer speaks each letter. I can read the entire page word by word or sentence by sentence. It will even speak as it goes through SpellChecker. It also incorporates a reading machine. Essentially, an item is scanned and then converted into synthesized speech. It can read a business card, a phone book, a newspaper, or a book. The computer will speak as it reads the printed material to you.

Blind Rehabilitation is much more than just using the skills and techniques to overcome blindness. It helps the "whole" person to adjust and deal with the challenges of losing sight. By gaining confidence, a person gains self-esteem. By overcoming limitations, one develops a positive self-image. While everyday challenges are still there, having the skills to deal with them help a person to deal with life.

I enjoyed learning to use the Perkins Braille Typewriter. My instructor, Harvey Lauer, is reading my paper with his fingers as I type.

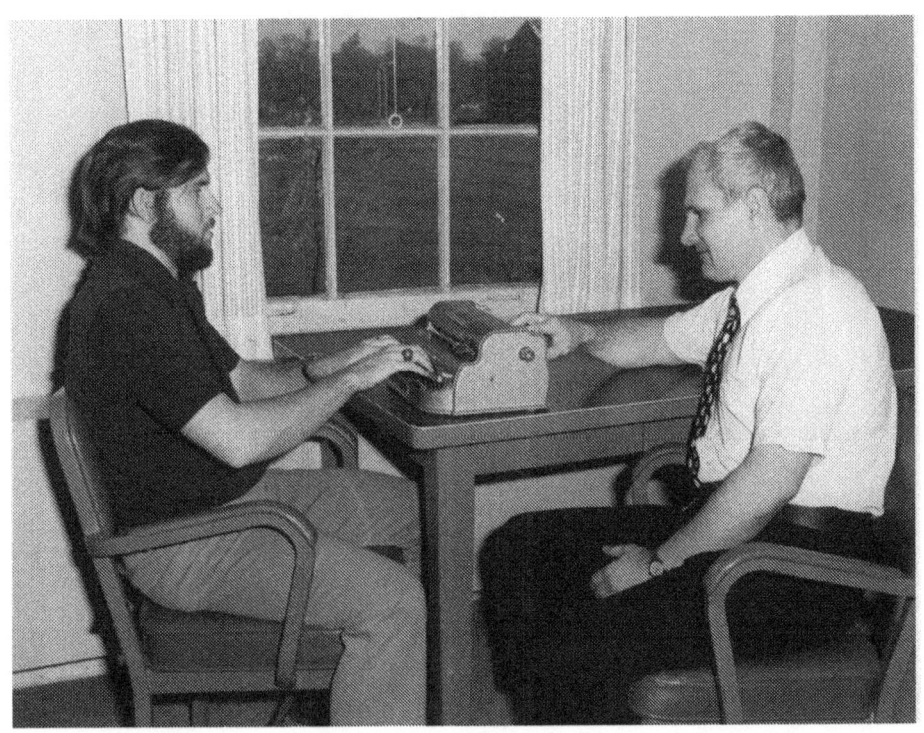

Chapter 6

"Adversity has the effect of eliciting talents, which in prosperous circumstances would have been dormant."

—*Horace*

Magic: The Amazing Haundini

There are very few blind magicians in the world. However, a blind magician introduced me to magic. When I was in the Veterans Hospital going through the Blind Rehabilitation program, I met Jerry Miller—stage name—Mr. Impossible. He was quite an excellent magician and performed many shows. After our classes at the hospital were finished, we would call a cab and go down to Mr. C's, a magic bar in Berwyn.

Magicians would come around to the tables and perform close-up magic. I remember this very well, and it was then and there that I decided I wanted to be a magician. It was interesting because Jerry would do magic for the magicians and they were amazed.

He was very good with coin magic, and his sleight of hand was quite excellent. Jerry also had a guide dog who was probably the best-trained dog I have ever come across. When I traveled with Jerry, I would hold on to his arm, and the dog would guide both of us. Once I dropped a pocket comb on the sidewalk. I was feeling around for it when the dog started nudging my hand with his head. He had the comb in his mouth and was trying to give it to me.

Eventually Jerry told me what to do to get started in magic. After I left the hospital, I went to a local magic shop and met the owner, Richard Gough. Rich was a professional magician (Riverboat Rich), and more importantly, was an excellent teacher of magic. He was very receptive to the idea of my wanting to learn magic. He first showed me some tricks that were "self-working." In other words, the apparatus did all the work. This was a good way for me to start putting together a routine.

My first shows were for my relatives and friends. It was very basic magic. After I became comfortable with my routine, I began doing shows at nursing homes and nursery schools. This was a great learning environment and confidence builder. My show consisted of the Magic Coloring Book (a coloring book that gets colored by "magic"), the Egg Bag routine (a classic of magic where an egg appears and disappears in an empty bag), Hippity Hop Rabbits (a black rabbit and a white rabbit change colors), and a production of candy.

Rich then began to teach me close-up magic. This is one of the most difficult forms of magic because your audience is seated right in front of you. Your sleights have to be perfect or you will ruin the effect of the trick. Without revealing the secret of any particular trick, Rich also taught me how to control a card. This is an important concept in doing card magic. As a blind magician, I am not able to "glimpse" at a card, so I must know ahead of time what I am dealing with. I would practice a certain "move" or sleight at least four hundred times before I would use it in a performance. It is difficult because it is hard for me to understand sometimes what the audience sees or must not see. Many magicians practice in front of a mirror, but that would not do me any good. Therefore, Rich would be my mirror and would tell me if I was "flashing" (showing a card or coin that should not be seen by the audience). He was a perfectionist, and he would not let me perform any trick when he thought I might be revealing the secret.

I also began to study many of the methods of the gamblers of the 1800s. Specifically, card cheaters. Many of the methods used by riverboat gamblers, mining town card sharks, and cowboy saloon dealers, lend themselves quite well to a blind magician. Imagine if you will, being able to "mark" a card so that you know what it is by feeling it. Suppose you are dealing and can feel the cards as fast as you deal them. Think of the possibilities—as you hold the deck and feel the bottom card and immediately know what it is. Now think of how great it would be to be able to "bottom deal" any card that you needed. These things are possible.

I should mention that no one could get away with "bottom dealing," "dealing seconds" (dealing the second card down instead of the top card), or marking a card in play, at a casino in Vegas. They are wise to these methods and could spot them right away. No. "Card punches," "crimps," and "rough sides," are things of a different era. While "strippers" (not the kind you're thinking of—this is a special type of marked card), and "short and long" cards have their place in magic, they have no place in today's high security casinos. I think it is also important to mention that a sighted magician can do miracles without the gimmicks, gaffs, and special methods that I might have to use to do the same effect.

I have been fortunate to know some really good magicians. They have taught me many of the effects I do today. Mike "Magic Mike"

Winters is a working professional. Of course, as with any good magician, Mike uses magic to entertain his audience. He projects his personality into each of his performances. He works everything from county fairs to school shows. He also studies magic and has many books on the different areas of magic. Magic Mike is also well known for his hypnosis routine.

One magician who has helped me in many of my routines is Bill "Magic 500" Hunter. Bill is one of the finest "walk-around" magicians in the country. His celebrity status comes from the fact that he has performed at the prestigious Indianapolis 500 for many years. AJ Foyt, Lloyd Ruby, Mario Andretti, Tom Sneva, and Al Unser (Sr. and Jr.) are but a few of the drivers Bill has entertained. Bill also performs at many corporate functions throughout the year. The Headline Prediction trick that I did on the Rosie O'Donnell show was taught to me by Bill. I should also mention that Bill is a fine golfer and has helped me to improve my game. He is great at lining me up before I hit the ball off the tee. It is only when we are playing for money that he lines me up facing the trees.

Some of the classic effects that I really like to perform are Macdonald's Aces and Matrix. In Macdonald's Aces, the four Aces are shown and then vanished and wind up under a spectator's hand. Matrix involves four cards and four coins. The coins are shown to be under each of the cards, but magically wind up all together under one card. I also like to end my close-up routine with the Sponge Balls. Basically, the sponge balls appear and disappear, and finally wind up in a spectator's hand.

It was also about the time I started classes in close-up magic that I began training with doves for my stage show. I loved working with doves as they are so beautiful to produce. After I would produce the bird, I would bring my hand up underneath him so that he would step up on my other hand. In doing this, the dove would flutter his wings.

The audience always loves to see this. Throughout my show I would produce a dove in many different ways. Sometimes from a single silk handkerchief and later from a pan full of fire. At the end of the show I would have seven doves in a beautiful birdcage. I would then cover up the cage with a silk. Next I would pick up the cage and toss it into the air. The silk would flutter to the ground—the cage and the doves had disappeared!

I would like to point out that I see magic as a method of entertaining people. When I perform magic, I want people to have fun. I want them to be entertained. I only wish I could see the reactions on their faces.

The Amazing Haundini and Gizmo, the magical rabbit. (Photo courtesy of Collins Photography)

I met Muhammad Ali at a magicians convention in Las Vegas. He loves magic, and especially enjoys doing magic for children in hospitals.

It was a great experience to be on the Rosie O'Donnell show. Rosie was in the film "A League of Their Own," which was about the Rockford Peaches. As I live in Rockford, I got Rosie a Rockford Peaches t-shirt that was signed by some of the original Rockford Peaches. Rosie loved it. Courtney Cox Arquette, who stars in the TV show "Friends," was also on the show.

Chapter 7

"The best and most beautiful things in the world cannot be seen or even touched, they must be felt with the heart."

"No pessimist ever discovered the secret of the stars, or sailed to an uncharted land, or opened a new doorway for the human spirit."

—Helen Keller

Gary Haun

The Magician and the Monkey Lady

It's interesting the way life brings us together with other people. It is much like two paths that cross in the middle of the woods. There are people walking in the same woods as us, but we only find this out when we meet at a crossing. In life, there are many people who have the same dreams and hopes as we do.

When I first decided to write to Dr. Jane Goodall, I had no idea who she was. I had heard her name on TV, and for some reason thought she had something to do with the "stray dogs of Africa." My dog, Duchess, had died and I felt really bad and wanted to write someone who would know how I felt. I then told someone I was going to write to Jane Goodall and they said, "Oh, she's the monkey lady."

I then read about Dr. Jane Goodall in the encyclopedia. What an amazing story. Her research has made her one of the world's most respected scientists. Internationally recognized as an expert in animal behavior, Dr. Goodall also leads the way in the conservation, preservation, and education of animals and environmental issues. She has lectured in just about every country on the planet, and has met with world leaders, animal researchers, and environmental scientists. Her concern for the environment extends far beyond that of the chimpanzees and Africa. It extends to all people and the whole world.

I am glad I did not write to Dr. Jane and ask her about "stray dogs or monkeys"! I did, however, write and ask for a letter or an autographed photo. I can still remember how excited I was when I received her reply. I was equally thrilled when she said that she would like to meet me. When I told my friend Roger about this, he could not believe it. He, as a wildlife photographer, knew a great deal about Dr. Jane's research with the chimpanzees of Gombe and of her concern for the environment. He was delighted when I told him that Jane had asked if we could come to the Roots and Shoots youth summit in Tulsa, Oklahoma.

Basically, Roots and Shoots is a program of the Jane Goodall Institute. Its purpose is to get children involved in doing positive activities for other people, for animals, and for the environment. The idea is that one positive action leads to another. Activities include volunteering to work in a local homeless shelter, planting trees in the community, helping out in an animal shelter, or starting a recycling program at school. These are but a few of the things that children are doing around the world in the Roots and Shoots program. I would like to see this program in every school in America. I think it would strengthen the community as children learned the positive aspects of doing for others.

When I first met Jane, it was as if I had known her all my life. She is one of the nicest, most caring persons I have ever met. I like the way she talks, with her gentle, but passionate voice. She speaks of hope and rainbows on cloudy days. She understands the beauty of an old oak tree, and she knows that dogs smile by wagging their tails. She listens to the heartbeat of animals and can hear them cry when they are mistreated. She is wise in the knowledge that one positive action can change the world.

Since that first meeting, I have come to know Dr. Jane far beyond her many highly respected awards and honors. Quite honestly, I do not know anything about chimpanzees. I don't know the difference between a monkey and a chimp or a gorilla and an orangutan. I do know, however, that a person like Dr. Jane comes along only once in a lifetime. And that meeting a person like her can make a difference in a person's life.

Jane is a real magician, as I define real magic—it is that which causes someone to care about someone or something enough to take action in a positive way. I have been at Jane's lectures where she has moved many to tears. She doesn't really lecture, she enlightens.

I could fill this entire book with chapters about Dr. Jane. The titles would be Compassion, Insight, Kindness, Spirituality, Charm, Sincerity, Hope and Charisma. Some people make this world a better place just by being who they are and by inspiring others to make this world a better place. Dr. Jane is that kind of person.

Through Dr. Jane, I know that once we have poured concrete on all our farmland and blacktop our grasslands, and cut down all our trees—the world will become an inhospitable place in which to live. I know that a negative attitude is like a cancer and that it will grow and grow until there is no hope for a cure. I know that a person who will mistreat an animal will surely have no problem in mistreating a human being. These are but a few things I have learned from Dr. Jane. Most importantly though, is the vision she has given to me. She has taught me, as well as thousands of others, that it is not so important what we see with our eyes—it is what we see with our hearts.

On a personal level, Dr. Jane is one of the most charming and interesting persons that I have ever met. On many occasions she will call me up and tell me about the places she is staying. She describes it much as a painter uses a canvas. She describes the colors, shapes, and unusual features of a building or the surroundings of a city. She has often called me while at an airport as she was waiting to catch her next flight. Of course she tells me how her mascot, Mister H, is getting along.

One of the things I treasure most are her letters to me. Specifically, letters that she wrote while she was at Gombe with her beloved chimpanzees. She has told me about them in a way that I know each of their personalities and special characteristics. From the letters you can feel the warmth and passion of this remarkable lady. What follows are a few of the letters that I hold very special.

> FROM THE PEAK—Gombe—14 July—2000
> Dear Gary,
>
> This is written from a very special place, on a very special day. Just so you know I am thinking of you—a very special person.
>
> 40 years ago on 14 July, Mum and I arrived for the first time on the Gombe beach. An infant chimpanzee lived in the forests, with her mother. Perhaps she watched my arrival from the safety of the trees. Her name was Fifi. Her mother was Flo.
>
> Waiting on the beach was a little boy of 7 years & his father. Rashidi took me for the first time into the forest to look for chimps—(I was made to take someone with me, by the Game Warden, who came to help set up our tent, then left).
>
> Jumanne helped Mum in her makeshift clinic—he pointed out the fisherman who rejoined the line, at the end, hoping for a second handout of aspirin & so forth.
>
> This morning, on this magic anniversary day, I spent time with FiFi—& <u>most</u> of her family. Her offspring—Freud, Fanni, Faustino, Ferdi & baby Flirt. And Fanni's two kids, Fudge & brand new 1 month

infant Fundi. Missing were Fifi's daughter Flosi who moved north, where she lives with her baby Forest. And—how lucky can you get—Frodo.

I also spent time with Jumanne. He went off to be a school teacher, but is badly low (since his father died & he had to look after the family). He is a part time accountant, & part time does Roots & Shoots.

I had to look at slides for a small celebration tonight. Just for Gombe Field Staff. Back to the early days. Infant Fifi, the one left alive from the early 60's. Old friend David Graybeard, Goliath, Mike, Flo. So many Individuals, loved, who are no longer with us. And of course, memories of Vanne are woven inextricably into the fabric of Gombe's history. So many, many memories. Bittersweet.

The long ago days can never return. But the future holds promise & especially you.

Love, Jane

Gombe 16-6-99
Dear Gary,

Just a wee note written on a piece of paper from my shirt pocket, left over from my chimp notes, from my own special piece of Paradise on Earth.

I've been following Gremlin and her adorable twins, Gold and Glitter. Gold is easy to recognize with her thick white beard. She's also more adventurous. But Glitter is a persistent little thing, and never gives up once she starts something.

6 year old sister Gaia adores them. Her idea of heaven is to play with, groom or carry one or other of them (they are 9 and 10 months now). Big brother Galahad (11) finds them very useful: if he wants to go somewhere and Gremlin won't follow, he just persuades a twin to cling onto him and sets off. Poor Gremlin has to follow.

I'm looking over Kasabret Valley. Gremlin and Glitter are lying in a big nest. Gaia is playing with Goldie nearby. Galahad is feeding. The sun is dropping down towards the mountains of Congo, so there is a shimmering red and gold pathway on the waters of the lake, down below, way below, Robin chats (def.-any of several birds with a chattering call) are singing their glorious song. Whistling in fact, in a duet.

We just had our first National Roots and Shoots Teacher Workshop. 95 teachers from 5 different parts of Tanzania, from 85 schools.

People said we'd get no more than 20 because we did not pay them any "sitting" or travel allowance, no per deim. But you see—they come because they love R and S (Roots and Shoots). In groups of 6 or 7, during 2 days, they visited Gombe—all but 6 saw at least me with chimps! They visited one school, tree nurseries and forestry projects, etc. learned how to use our NEW R+S teacher manual. Talks by Dr. Jane, And they had FUN. So successful that UNICEF will fully fund a Regional Conference in September—and include teachers from the several big refugee camps in the Rigowa region.

Well, I must go on down now and swim in the lake. So beautiful, so much clean clear water. Just wanted you to know I'm thinking of you here.

Much Love—Jane

Gombe 14 July 98

It was such a surprise to hear your voice last week! * (I called Jane at Dar es Salaam, Tanzania). Great! I'm just dropping you a line because we finally made it to Gombe—mixture of commercial and charter plane—& boat as usual. And today, 2nd day here is so exciting! Gremlin turned up with TWINS!!! The third pair in 38 years. It was Gremlin's mother, Melista who had the first known twins. Of whom one, Gimble, survived. Gremlin is Goblin's young sister & has 2 other kids. Ghastly, but Fifi and daughter Farri tried to kill the twins—inexplicable. Dad Gremlin won out & all is well.

Lots of love—Jane

2 June 99

Dearest Gary,

In the car on the way to Mozambique. Just 6 days. It was great talking with you—in Dar and the UK. This is a picture of the teacher who needs the blind (Braille) watch. Have you heard anything of the little boy in New Jersey who suddenly went blind.

Talk soon, Love, Jane

From the Birches (Jane's home in England)
Dear Gary,

What a truly amazing person you are. As you know, you make such an impact, your life is an inspiration to everyone. The moment I got your second letter I knew that it would be a fabulous experience for my Roots Shoots kids, I knew it would fit right in with our philosophy.

But I had no way of knowing just what a delightful and lovely person you truly are.

I cannot thank you enough for coming to Tulsa. Your presence, your show, just made all the difference. Even if you were a lousy magician it would have been fabulous—but on top of everything else, you are a brilliant magician. I imagine you have reached the very top of your art!

And now, I am on a plane flying through the night from London to Uganda. We landed in Nairobi at 3:00 AM. Horrid time.—and just now taking off for Entebbe,—where I do a Wildlife Awareness Week. Then Ethiopia & talk to the teachers of the International Schools of Eastern Africa. Then Nairobi to visit our chimps sanctuary. Then Ghana—first schools of Western Africa, then, to the Peace Summit in LA!

Anyway, so many Thanks, much admiration,

Love, Jane

25 March 1999

Just to let you know I'm thinking of you, sitting on my veranda, looking out over the Nile. This conference, 3 days, allowed me a free day, in the middle, so I could see the PYRAMIDS & the Sphinx. Amazing! Was sorry for camels—DID NOT RIDE ONE! But it felt like being in a history book, I always loved Egyptian history. They were amazing. See you soon—love, Jane

Bournemouth, The Birches 27 June 1999

Just a note. I traveled on a plane from Scotland with a blind man & his dog, Dee. A beautiful dog, she was. Anyway, of course, I went over & said hello, and introduced him to Mister H. I know he'd like a note from you.

Love, Jane.

Dr. Jane's message of hope is *"One person can make a difference."* She has touched the lives of so many in so many different ways. Her enlightened spirit reaches out to all of God's creatures and His creations.

Chapter 8

"The greatest discovery of my generation is that a human being can alter his life by altering his attitude."
—William James

The Magic of Mister H

On April 28th, 1995, I presented Dr. Jane Goodall with a very special stuffed animal. It was a furry, monkey-like creature with a banana and a silly, but infectious smile. When I gave it to Dr. Jane, I told her that I thought it was a chimpanzee. After all, the catalog that I ordered it from plainly stated it was—Chimpanzee with banana. Dr. Jane was quite amused, and said in her very soft-spoken English accent, "Gary, this doesn't look like a chimp at all." I simply replied, "How would you know?" We both still laugh about this.

I was very honored when Dr. Jane named the brown-fur, big-tail, banana-eating, silly-grinning creature after me. She named him Mister H. Mister H has a special kind of magic...the magic of Hope...of Heart...of Happiness. Maybe that's what the H really stands for. Mister H has touched the lives of many, especially children. He has been touched by children who are blind, in wheelchairs, deaf, and some who are terminally ill.

One child held on to Mister H until he died. Dr. Jane had visited the child and told him that Mister H was magical and that he would help comfort him. Mister H did just that. I received a letter from the family of the child, and they said that Mister H seemed to bring a certain peacefulness to the child.

Mister H is also somewhat of an ambassador of hope. Dr. Jane has introduced him to thousands of people in many different countries. He has met with the President of the United States as well as several heads of state from countries around the world. Mister H has traveled thousands of miles and been to places like Buckingham Palace and the Great Pyramids of Egypt. Through it all he keeps smiling!

In Japan Dr. Jane visited a childrens hospital. Many of the children had cancer and some were very sick. After telling the children about Mister H, they all wanted to touch this fuzzy friend of Dr. Jane's. The children's faces lit up, many smiled, and many said that they could feel the magic of Mister H.

Mister H always smiles no matter what the situation is. Maybe there's something we could learn here. A smile seems to help others sometimes. Try it. Mister H smiles no matter who he meets. There might be a lesson here also. Whether it's a sick child in Africa or the

President of the United States, we are all part of the human race. With all our differences we are all very much the same. We may have different dreams, but basically it comes down to what makes us happy. It has been said that the highest level of sophistication is being able to deal with all people on all levels. Mister H does this with a simple smile.

It would seem that as long as Mister H has his banana, he is happy. I believe the saying "He who is rich is he who has few wants," applies here. Granted, we all need more than a banana in today's society, but maybe our lives would be simpler if we didn't need so many bananas to keep us happy.

There is a little of Mister H in all of us. It begins with a smile.

Dr. Jane Goodall with Mister H.

Chapter 9

"When one door closes another door opens; but we so often look so long and so regretfully upon the closed door, that we do not see the ones which open for us."
—Alexander Graham Bell

The Great Horndini

The Lindsay Wildlife Museum in California is a very special place. The museum's Wildlife Hospital treats nearly 7,000 injured and orphaned animals every year. The animals that cannot be released back into the wild become part of the museum. The animals then become an important part of the Lindsay Museum educational exhibits.

There is a great horned owl who lives at the museum. He is a very proud and majestic bird and looks every bit the part of "the wise old owl." He is very pretty, with his many different colored feathers and he moves his head in the very "owl-like" side-to-side motion. He is blind.

It seems the owl flew into the very sharp spines of a cactus and was blinded immediately. He is cared for by the volunteers at the museum. The owl is doing fine and has adjusted remarkably well to his new home.

Dr. Jane Goodall visited the museum and was quite taken by this beautiful animal. She asked what the owl's name was. It was explained that the animals are not given names, as that may imply that these animals are like pets. Since hundreds of people visit the museum, the educational thrust is to connect and respect the natural habitat of the animals. Understandably, animals in their natural environment do not have names like we do. They only have names after "we" give them a name.

Dr. Jane's point of view is somewhat different. If we name the animals, they become not pets, but our friends. As a matter of fact, Jane has names for all the chimps at Gombe. So it was, that this insight was accepted, and Dr. Jane had the honor of naming this magnificent owl. She told the directors of the museum about me and that my magician name was "the Amazing Haundini." Since the owl was a great horned owl, his name would be "The Great Horndini."

I have found a kindred spirit in this owl. And I mean just that—spirit. For this owl, although blinded, knows he's still an owl. Just as I, although blind, still know I am the person I always was. Everyone who has told me about this owl has used the terms proud and dignified. He has adjusted well and is happy. I suppose all of us can learn from the wise old owl.

Dr. Jane gave me a feather from this owl. Some college students who volunteer at the museum gave me a few more at the Dallas College Roots and Shoots Summit. I often touch these feathers, and this gives me strength. Strength to never give up, strength to do the best I can, strength to fly to new heights. Just like the owl, I know I have limitations, but my "flight wings" work just fine.

I was honored to have this owl named after me. After all, he is magical. As I've said before, real magic is that which makes people feel positive and inspires them to take a positive action. When facing adversity, knowing who and what you are, is certainly something the wise old owl can teach us.

The Great Horndini (Photo courtesy of Lindsay Museum)

Chapter 10

"Remember that if the opportunities for great deeds should never come, the opportunities for good deeds are renewed day by day. The thing for us to long for is the goodness, not the glory."

—*F. W. Faber*

Sharing the Vision...

The only real adventure is that of life. To be more specific—the adventure of life is in sharing the vision with others. I personally gain satisfaction and a sense of well being when I feel I have helped someone in some way. It doesn't have to be a big enlightenment to the other person, only that it brings some light into their life. It is not about being a good person; it's about being good to someone else.

I was hesitant to write this chapter as I truly believe that a person must do good deeds in an anonymous way. I do not seek awards, plaques, or praise from others. I take comfort in knowing that I've done my best, and that is enough. However, I was encouraged by others to talk about the way I have influenced others in a positive way. I would hope that in doing so it would cause others to reflect upon what they may be able to do.

Of the many ways to "share the vision," one of the most important is to help someone who is physically, mentally, or spiritually in a valley. When I say spiritually, I do not mean it in a religious way. I am talking about the human spirit—the will to go on in life. Some people cannot see light at the end of the tunnel. They think they are in a cave with no chance of ever getting out. I have written to many people who were in this condition. A letter can be a powerful connection and actually be a life preserver to many. Sometimes encouragement or even a kind word is enough for a person to reflect upon.

I have many people who contact me in this regard. They know of someone who needs help. Dr. Jane Goodall has called me on several occasions asking if I could write or call someone she has met during her many travels. Of the thousands of people she meets each year, she is especially concerned with those in need. Not in need of material things, but of those in need of "a positive action." As Dr. Jane says, "A positive action will in turn lead to a positive action." She not only believes in this philosophy, she lives it. I try to live it too.

Over the years I have contacted people who are blind, terminally ill, depressed, paralyzed, or who have some life-threatening condition. I usually call the person and then follow up with a letter. In many instances I talk to the parents of a child who is very sick. This is rather difficult as I think of how I would feel if my son were in that situation. It seems to make people feel better if they know someone really cares about them. I think it is much like the feeling of holding someone's hand during a difficult time.

On many occasions I am asked to give technical assistance. This is usually to other blind people. I am knowledgeable as to the many aids and appliances that are available to the blind. Many blind people do not have the resources to investigate what is available to them. I have also helped many blind high school students with their decisions about college. I usually get questions on reader services, text on cassette tape, recorder usage, advanced note-taking methods, and computer technology (talking or synthesized speech computers).

In certain instances, I will actually send aids and appliances to those who cannot get them from other sources. For example, Dr. Goodall recently told me of a blind teacher whom she met in a village in Africa. The teacher taught blind children from the surrounding areas. He had heard about Braille watches but had never had one. I told Dr. Jane I would take care of it and sent a new Braille watch to give to the teacher. While a new watch may not seem much to many, to a few it can be one of the greatest things in life.

I have also sent many things to people who are newly blind. Many times they do not know what is available to them. They are relieved to know there are aids that will make their life easier. I have sent out several talking calculators, talking clocks, and talking watches. I also like sending marking devices such as Braille dots and tactile markers to be used on microwave ovens, washing machines, thermostats, dishwashers, and many other devices. These are simple solutions to problems that many newly-blinded people encounter.

I have also sent out many unusual or hard-to-get items that a blind person might need. A Braille compass is a perfect example. I know that as a blind scuba diver, I could not have passed my certification without using a Braille compass. As more and more blind people are becoming interested in scuba diving, I am often asked to find them a Braille compass. I also assist them by explaining about talking or audible dive computers and other assistive technology.

One of the more rewarding experiences I have had is in counseling the parents of blind children. I let them know of the many opportunities that are available to their child. Also, I let them know about my many experiences and adventures, and that just because someone is blind, it doesn't mean an unfulfilled life. I also share my experiences, and those of other blind people, with blind children and young adults. It is not a mater of "how do you scuba dive" or "how do you climb to the summit of a great mountain," but more importantly, "I am able to do these things and so are you if you have the desire."

Periodically, I send certain items to children in Africa. Many children who live in remote villages are in desperate need of ink pens and school supplies. Sometimes I contact companies and corporations that are willing to donate large amounts of ink pens. I will then send these to people who are actually traveling to Africa and who will personally give these items to the children. I suppose I like the idea that in some way this makes the world a little bit smaller and somehow brings us closer together.

I also quite often send Braille paper and Braille writing devices to different areas of the world. In many countries these items are very difficult to obtain. Once again I feel there is some connection when I know these items are being used to help another blind person learn a new skill and something that is going to make their life a little bit easier.

I suppose that through Mister H and Dr. Jane, I have touched the lives of thousands of people. At the very least, maybe giving them a sense of hope and positive direction. At the very best, I hope their lives are made better, and somehow they will in turn be able to touch the life of someone else. In this way the circle never ends.

Chapter 11

"Be not afraid of going slowly; be afraid only of standing still."

—Chinese Proverb

"The people who get on in this world are the people who get up and look for the circumstances they want, and if they don't find them, make them."

—George Bernard Shaw

Martial Arts: Of Katas, Kamas and Kumite

I began studying the martial arts when I was in the Marine Corps. Just about every Marine base I was stationed at had a karate or judo club. Although the instruction was quite excellent, I was never stationed at one base long enough to become proficient at the art.

Interestingly enough my intense pursuit of the martial arts began after I lost my eyesight. I was living in Oak Ridge, Tennessee, at the time and had recently returned from blind rehabilitation training at the veterans hospital. With my newfound confidence in myself, I enrolled in college and also wanted to rekindle my interest in the martial arts.

Quite honestly, I just wanted to get into a form of exercise that would help me stay in shape. As I was familiar with the exercises in the martial arts, I thought karate would be the best avenue of approach. I did not know at the time that this avenue would be a road I would follow the rest of my life.

I contacted the local karate school and explained my situation. I told the instructor that I just wanted to do the exercises such as punching, kicking, and stretching. With no hesitation whatsoever, the instructor told me to meet him before classes the next day. I suppose that for some reason, I had thought my being blind would have initiated more questions. This was my introduction into what I now call "falling prey to my own limitations." Sometimes people with limitations doubt themselves so much that they make the limitations a problem before they ever try anything. In this case I almost talked myself out of going to the karate school. Why did I ever think I could do this? I would only disappoint myself. What if...and then it stopped. I made a choice. If I don't go, I will be doubting myself for the rest of my life.

The next day I went to the karate school. I was introduced to *Sensei* (teacher) Wayne Brooks, the instructor for the Harold Long School of Karate. I liked Wayne immediately.

It was not so much for what he said, it was for what he didn't say. Although I was his first blind student, Wayne did not consider blindness an issue. In fact, he seemed quite happy to have me as a student, and was very positive about me being in the class.

He gave me a black *gi* (karate uniform) and a white *obi* (belt). After putting on the gi, Wayne walked me around the *dojo* (training facility) and introduced me to a few of the other students. We then went to an area and began a series of exercises. I know this may seem crazy, but the intense workout made me feel very, very happy. I don't know what it was. I think it was because at that moment, I didn't think about being blind. I wasn't feeling sorry for myself. I was feeling good about myself.

After several weeks of doing exercises, Wayne asked me if I would like to learn an *Isshinryu kata*. *Isshinryu* karate is an Okinawan style of karate. It is different from other forms of karate, and is characterized by its use of the vertical fist and short, powerful kicks. *Isshinryu Katas* (prearranged forms) have many movements, most with many different kicks and punches. However, one of the forms must be done very slowly, and each movement is done in a very methodical manner. *Sanchin kata* is a form that is distinguished by its deep breathing on every movement. For example, a movement begins by breathing in. Not a normal inhalation, but breathing in very deeply. Then, while punching very, very slowly—exhaling out. In all my years of training in the martial arts, I believe the *Sanchin kata* is the most important. It is also one of the hardest to perform.

Sanchin was, and still is, the only *kata* I would learn in *Isshinryu*. Most students in karate learn one *kata* and then go on to the next higher level *kata*. However, Wayne knew that it might be difficult for me to learn too many *katas*, and in the process, not do them well. I can still recall Wayne saying, "A smart fox doesn't chase two rabbits at once." No. Wayne knew that if I could learn this one *kata*, and learn to do it well, that it would help me to learn other things in my life.

I suppose for many people, doing one *kata* over and over again, would be boring. I am sure the repetition of doing a *kata* like *Sanchin*, with its slow, deliberate movements would tax the attention span of most. I, however, felt better each and every time I went through the form. I could tell that I was getting stronger, and I was becoming more confident that I was performing this kata as it was supposed to be done. Wayne must have thought the same thing, because he told me I was ready to compete in a karate tournament.

Karate tournaments usually consists of *kumite* (free-sparring or fighting), *kata* (forms), and sometimes breaking (board or brick breaking competition) and weapons (martial arts weapons). There are divisions for each belt level. Not all karate schools have the same belt structure (kung fu schools have sashes). One school might progress from white, orange, green, brown, and black. Another school might have white, yellow, green, blue, brown, red, and black belts. However, in a tournament, most ability levels are grouped together. I was in a unique position. I was a white belt doing a high level *kata*.

When my name was announced, you could have heard a pin drop. Wayne led me to the starting position. I bowed to the judges and asked them for permission to remove my *gi* top. This is allowed when performing the *Sanchin kata,* so that the judges may see your breathing technique. I removed and folded my *gi* top very carefully. I then knelt down and set my *gi* on the floor. I stood up, bowed once again to the judges, and began the *kata*.

There is no better feeling in life than when you're doing something well; almost, and I say this with the utmost humility, to a state of perfection. When I finished, the entire audience, as well as the other competitors, gave me a standing ovation. It went on for several minutes. It was almost like being in a movie. I took first place in the tournament, but more importantly than that, I learned a lesson that would follow me the rest of my life. If you want to do something well, you must work at it. If you want to achieve a goal, you will find a way to do it. I believe that *Sensei* Brooks knew all along that this was the karate lesson he wanted me to learn.

One day in class, Wayne said he wanted me to learn some self-defense. He said he had given some thought as to the best way to teach me to fight. I had fought when I was in the Marines, but this was something entirely different. Wayne put on a pair of boxing gloves and told me he was going to hit me. He did. It wasn't hard, but it got my immediate attention. He then said he was going to hit me again. He did. Again in the face, and a little bit harder. Wayne said he was going to hit me again. This time, with no hesitation, I put my hands up over my face to block the punch.

Wayne had found the key to making me understand what it means to cover up when fighting. Eventually Wayne proceeded to throw in some kicks to my ribs. I was now listening to his every movement, and knew I had to react very quickly. These exercises quickened my reflexes to a point where I could effectively block a kick or a punch. As soon as I was punched, I would immediately punch back and usually follow up with a kick. Of course the downside to this strategy was that I usually had to take a punch before I gave one out. Needless to say, the one I gave out had to be a good one.

I would take about five hits to every one I gave out. I also developed a strong side kick that usually backed off the opponent right away. In demonstrations I would break concrete blocks and bricks with this single sidekick. The more experience I had with fighting, the more confident I became. I would later teach other blind people the same way that Wayne had taught me.

Along with increasing reaction time and reflexes, the other benefits of the martial arts apply to both blind and sighted. However, some are especially beneficial to the blind. Balance, coordination, strength, and flexibility can be an asset in orientation and mobility.

Uneven stairs, unlevel terrain, and unexpected obstacles can sometimes be difficult situations. I'm happy that over the years there has been a huge increase in the number of visually-impaired people training in the martial arts. I hope this trend continues.

When I moved back to Illinois, I knew I wanted to take karate lessons again. I contacted Master Young Hong at the Young Hong Karate Institute. Master Hong taught Korean Tae Kwon Do, which is a very different style than the Okinawan *Isshinryu*. I loved learning Tae Kwon Do. Master Hong was a very patient instructor, and would physically put my arms and feet in the correct position for each move.

I was still a white belt when Master Hong asked me to go to a karate tournament. I knew only one *kata*, but like the *Sanchin kata*, I had practiced it many times. Tae Kwon Do *katas* use quick powerful punches and high kicks. I placed first in the tournament, but more importantly gained some good experience about tournaments. You must "center" yourself before performing your *kata*. That is, visualize yourself doing the *kata* and also mentally eliminate any distractions. This process would serve me well dealing with other matters, and I still feel this is another one of those "lessons for life."

I trained with Master Hong for five years, and I would train four to five times a week. I advanced through the belt ranks at an advanced pace. I progressed from white to orange, yellow, green, blue, and then to brown. Brown belt is an advanced rank and everyone trains very hard, as their next rank is the coveted black belt. Master Hong had two degrees of brown belt and then red belt. The red belt signifies your next rank is black belt. As a red belt, you are now helping to teach others. I enjoyed helping others to learn.

My black belt test was very tough. I had to do all the *katas* for each of the belt ranks, plus the advanced black belt *katas*. I had to break several boards with multiple kicks and punches. I also broke two concrete bricks. Then I had to free-fight someone who was physically larger than I was. I then had to fight two opponents at once. As you can imagine, this was very difficult for me, but the years of training paid off. I was promoted to black belt after the test.

I continued training with Master Hong until I earned my second-degree black belt. By this time I had been to over 100 tournaments. I enjoyed Tae Kwon Do but wanted to learn martial arts weaponry. I then began training with *Shihan* Ed Stiltner who ran a local karate school. *Shihan* (master) Stiltner taught an Okinawan style of karate very similar to *Isshinryu*.

I also began attending many seminars at this time. I attended one that featured Bill "Superfoot" Wallace and an old friend of mine, Dale Kirby. I had met Dale when I lived in Tennessee. He is an expert at Japanese swordsmanship. In fact it was from this acquaintance that I became interested in the sword. I also attended a seminar taught by Stephen K. Hayes, who teaches *Ninjutsu*. Stephen had trained with Grandmaster Masaaki Hatsumi in Japan. The two skills I found most interesting were *Ninjutsu* sword techniques and perception training. This last skill involved increasing kinesthetic perception to the point that you could sense the movement of a person who was behind you. Blind people have an increased sense of kinesthetic perception that helps to sense people or objects that are close to them. Some call this "human radar," and although everyone has this sense, as a blind person, I rely on it more than a sighted person would need to.

Through *Shihan* Stiltner, I met and began training with Dr. Rod Sacharnoski, founder of Juko Kai International. Dr. Sacharnoski holds many degrees in many different martial arts. He is also the founder of *Juko Kai Ki* Power training. *Ki* is an internal energy that, once mastered, enables a person to absorb full power punches or kicks without injury. Dr. Sacharnoski teaches jujutsu, judo, karate, and many different weapon arts.

I began taking jujutsu with Dr. Sacharnoski. I must admit that this is the most physically demanding art I have ever studied. It can be brutally painful. There are many wristlocks and throws that one must endure when practicing this art. Being thrown over someone's shoulder was, at first, very difficult to master. Needless to say, because I am blind, I did not know when I was about to hit the ground. Usually the student slaps his arm and *kiais* (yells) to absorb the shock of the fall. In my case I would hit the ground and just yell from the pain.

I then began studying *Hanbo-jutsu* which is Japanese stick fighting. This is well-suited for the blind as it involves the use of a stick about the same size as a mobility cane. I liked this art so much that I would study it for years and also became graded as a black belt.

I also studied *Kobujutsu*, which is Okinawan weaponry. The five main weapons of this art are the *sai* (a small pitchfork-like weapon), the *kama* (a sharp-bladed sickle), the *tonfa* (a wooden board with a handle), *nunchuka* (two pieces of wood tied together with a rope or chain), and the *bo* staff (a long wooden staff). What is interesting about these weapons is that they were originally farm implements. The Okinawan farmers adapted them as weapons to fight invaders. Part of the training is how to use them to defend against an opponent with a samurai sword. I would also stay with this art until I was graded as a black belt in it.

I began studying *iaijutsu* (pronounced *ee-eye-jut-soo*) with the sword class that Dr. Sacharnoski taught. I always wanted to learn more about the sword, and loved sword class. I then began taking private lessons to gain further insight, and intense training in the sword. Sword training was very different from all the other styles of martial arts I had studied.

Essentially, *iaijutsu* is centered around the basic movements of *nukidashi* (drawing the blade from the scabbard), *chiburi* (deblooding the blade after a cut), and *noto* (sheathing the blade). These movements, combined with the many different types of cuts, make *iaijutsu* one of the most interesting martial arts one can ever study. There are no belt levels in *iaijutsu*, but instead there are licenses. I would train with the sword until I reached the *Menkyo Shihan* level (licensed Master Instructor). The licenses had to come from Japan. I still practice the sword today and study samurai history.

Due to the intense concentration required, the mind is constantly active. The swordsman is always searching for a state of perfection with the sword. This art has been passed down for hundreds of years but the goal remains the same. Constant improvement, both physically and mentally.

A healthy mental attitude leads to a positive self-image—something that is sometimes lacking inside many people, both blind and sighted. Just as it has helped me to deal with everyday stress and frustration, I believe sword training could help many others. I have applied the confidence I have gained from sword training to many areas of my life. I have used it in facing new challenges—slicing away difficulty, much like making cuts with the sword. I mentally try to cut away obstacles, problems, and obstructions that lie in the "pathway of possibilities."

Sword training has taught me persistence and dedication. You cannot give up or you will never achieve your goal. Upon reflection, this is probably true of many things in life. Sometimes we need to mentally cut away the imperfect parts to find out the "real." Instant enlightenment is indeed rare.

The days of mortal combat with swords are gone. However, the lessons learned from this ancient art are many. Personally, it has helped me to focus on goals and objectives. And more importantly, I have learned a positive way of thinking to overcome an opponent that is very much a reality in today's society—negativity. *Iaijutsu* is alive and well.

Gary Haun

I have competed in over 100 karate tournaments. In 1978 I won the Weapons Division at a tournament held at the Playboy Club in Lake Geneva, Wisconsin. It was a memorable awards presentation.

Chapter 12

"It is better to live one year in the life of a tiger, than to live a thousand years in the life of a sheep."

—*Tibetan proverb*

Gary Haun

Skydiving: The Moment of Truth

"Why would any one want to jump out of a perfectly good airplane?" When I speak of skydiving, someone usually asks this question.

I talked about it for years. I always wanted to go. It was just that I had so many questions about it. The number one question was "Is it safe?" I also wanted to know if there was a way I would be able to do it. There was. I had heard about tandem skydiving from a friend. I was competing in a 10k foot race in Lake Geneva, Wisconsin. Several people from the local running club had gone skydiving. They talked about it with excitement and exhilaration. They encouraged me to contact the skydiving facility.

My friend Roger had also been skydiving and wanted to go again. At the time, I was training for a marathon, and my running partner, Terri Gray, also expressed a desire to go skydiving. I know this sounds crazy, but I took comfort in the fact that Terri would be going along with us. Terri is a nurse, and I thought that if the parachute didn't open, she would be there to fix me up. I know…I know.

I contacted the Sky Knights Skydiving Facility in East Troy, Wisconsin, and set up a date. On a beautiful Saturday morning, we got an early start and were the first group of people to arrive at the small airport. I was surprised at how laid back everyone was. This made me feel very comfortable. I then asked one of the ladies who worked at the Sky Knights facility if she knew of a man named Mark Krause. I told her that my friends said that I should jump with him, if that was possible. She said, "Why don't you ask him? He's standing right beside you." Mark laughed and introduced himself. He had a great sense of humor, and I immediately liked him.

Mark had over 4,000 jumps. I liked his attitude and the way he explained what was going to happen. The confidence in his voice made me feel very comfortable, and I can truthfully say that I was not nervous or scared at this point. I think it was a matter of listening to every word and paying close attention to Mark's instructions. Mark went through the procedure for exiting the plane. On a tandem jump, the instructor is linked to your back by locking buckles. Mark told me not to worry about anything, and just enjoy the experience. It seems he had enough confidence for both of us, and that was good. Since he was connected to me, I knew that he wanted me to have a safe jump.

I would be the first jumper of the day. Mark had me put on a jumpsuit and then he put the tandem harness on me. We then walked out to the airplane, and Mark once again went through the procedure for getting out of the plane. He told me that if there was anything else I needed to know, he would tell me on the way down. At this time I was introduced to the cameraman, who would be filming my jump, and also introduced to the pilot. Mark sensed my uneasiness when I heard the door shut and immediately began asking me questions. I knew he was doing this to get my mind off the negative and on to the positive. "Gary, you're gonna love this!" Then the pilot started the engine and began to taxi down the runway. At this time I remember hoping that I had been a good person and kind to animals.

It took the plane several minutes to gain altitude. On the way up, Mark was still asking me questions and talking as if we were at home sitting on the patio. This had a very calming effect on me. It really took my mind off the fact that I was in an airplane that was on its way to 13,000 feet. Mark was really great at bringing the negative intensity level down. He kept saying, "Just another day at the office."

It took us about 20 minutes to reach our jump altitude. Then things started to happen. The cameraman moved up to the side door to open it up. The sound of the air rushing by the airplane is incredible. This really gets your attention. It also gets your adrenaline pumping. Although I could not see this, the cameraman actually exits the airplane and holds on to the wing. This way he can get a picture of you exiting the airplane. When I was told about this later, I was totally amazed.

Then Mark moved behind me and clipped himself to my back. He then spoke some words that I will never forget. "Gary, we're locked, cocked, and ready to rock!" And in a very methodical manner, we both leaned forward toward the open door. With the wind roaring by us at what seemed to be a million miles an hour, Mark guided my leg to place my foot on the little square platform under the door. The wind immediately blew my leg away from the platform. At first this startled me, but Mark, in a very calm and reassuring voice said, "Gary—keep your foot down on the platform."

Next, came what I call the moment of truth. I had to reach out and grab the strut of the wing. I had always thought that this would be the time I might have problems with. I had thought how embarrassing it would be for them to have to land the plane with me halfway out the door and my hand frozen to the wing strut. I pictured someone having to use a crowbar to pry my hand off the airplane, and an imprint of my hand pressed into the wing.

However, none of this came to be because of Mark's insight and professional experience. The split second Mark guided my hand to the strut, I steadied myself for a moment—and then Mark rolled us forward.

Ladies and gentlemen, I want to tell you this is an incredible feeling. I would like to say exiting the airplane is another moment of truth, but it happens so quickly that you don't have time to think about it. Right after we rolled out, it seemed as if we tumbled, as if we were doing a somersault. Actually, we just turned over to begin our free fall. Mark told me to put my arms out to the sides and enjoy it. In free fall you are descending at a speed of 120 miles per hour. However, I felt like I was flying straight out and never sensed falling down. I am sure that blindness has something to do with this, as I could not see the ground. It feels as if you are flying through the air like Superman. I actually felt like Superman. That's right. At that particular moment, I was "flying through the air like a speeding bullet."

I think the best way to describe free fall is a total sensory overload. A maximum emotional experience. It's almost surrealistic, as if being in a dream. I absolutely loved it. At about 10,000 feet, Mark told me to wave to the cameraman who was right out in front of us. He told me not to be startled, but the cameraman was coming over to touch us. This is such a great feeling. Being at 10,000 feet in the sky and having someone come over to shake your hand. Wow!

As soon as the cameraman backed away, Mark shifted the weight of his body. By doing this, we made a turn. He then turned us back the other way. All through these maneuvers, I still felt as if I were flying straight out. Actually, we had dropped from 13,000 feet to 5,000 feet in about 40 seconds. Mark then told me he was going to pull the ripcord. This may seem strange, but I did not feel the parachute open. I sensed we were slowing down, but I did not know the chute had opened. I asked Mark if the parachute was open. He said yes, but for some reason I asked him again. "Gary, I can see it! We got a good canopy." I believe that I was on such a high from the free fall that I did not realize we were now slowly dropping straight down.

Mark then gave me our landing instructions. I was to pull my knees back to my chest and Mark would tell me when to set my feet down. As soon as he said, "OK, pull your knees up to your chest," I felt the parachute slow, and within seconds Mark said, "Put your feet down, we've landed." I don't know what I had expected on the landing. I guess I thought too much about the paratroopers in the military, who would land and roll on the ground. No, it was nothing like that. In fact, it was like landing on a pillow.

Mark then quickly unsnapped the buckles that held us together. I was still in a state of euphoria. I turned and gave Mark a hug and thanked him for this experience. Roger and Terri were there to greet me. I couldn't tell them enough how incredible this was. I was happy that they too, would experience this. I was so happy. It definitely was the thrill of a lifetime.

Chapter 13

"Life is either a daring adventure or nothing."

—Helen Keller

Up. Up and Away

The gentle giants. A ride in a hot air balloon is pure magic. They float along the wind currents like huge multi-colored Christmas ornaments filled with helium. There is no helium needed for a hot air balloon though, only hot air. The principle of a hot air balloon is simple enough. Hot air rises. Capture the hot air in a balloon and it will rise—carrying the basket of people with it.

I had always wanted to go up in a hot air balloon. I had seen them when I had my eyesight, but never actually had an opportunity to go up in one. They seemed so mystical, so enchanting, and so free-spirited. I remembered it was the mode of transportation for Dorothy and the Wizard to get them back home to Kansas. When I reflect back to my thoughts of what a hot air balloon looked like, I envision huge marbles in the sky.

On a fine April morning in Waterloo, Iowa, I would fulfill the dream. Along with five of my good friends, I was there to take in the Waterloo Days Hot Air Balloon Rally. It was a festival atmosphere. There was the smell of hot dogs, pork chop sandwiches, and cotton candy. There was the sound of the vendors selling everything from t-shirts to souvenir drinking cups. It was an event that was being enjoyed by all types of people, young and old, and from many different areas of the country.

In the afternoon, after we had sampled many of the liquid refreshments at the festival, we decided we would try to line up a balloon ride. I think it had something to do with the liquid refreshments. We were all in a festival mood and decided to throw caution to the winds—literally.

We went to one of the balloon teams and asked them if we could go up for a ride. We found out that hot air balloons fall (no pun intended) under the legal guidelines of the FAA (Federal Aviation Administration), and that certain requirements are in force for those carrying passengers. Also, some balloons could only carry one or two people. Along with myself, there was Roger, his sisters Debbie and Darla, Darla's husband Jim, and Paul Nelson. We knew now that we would have to talk to someone with a big balloon.

In time we came across a team of balloonists from California. One couple had a huge balloon. We talked to the pilot and he said he could take us up—if we became part of the crew. This meant we would have to help him get the balloon up at the start, and fold it up when we finished the ride. Also, the basket could hold only six people so Paul decided he would go with the chase crew. This is the truck that follows the balloon around so it is there at the end of the flight.

The first thing to be done was to take the folded balloon off the truck and to roll it out on the ground. There were going to be about 60 balloons going up that day, so we went to an area reserved for the different balloon teams. When many balloons go up at once it is called a mass ascension. Once the balloon is rolled out, you really get a good idea of how big it is. Ron, our pilot, wanted me to be very involved in the operation. He was great at explaining every little detail of what we were doing. He had me feel the balloon envelope (which is essentially the balloon itself), and he walked me along the edge so I could get a feel for how big the balloon was. The envelope is made of a material that feels like nylon and silk. It is very light but also very durable. There is a flap at the top that can be pulled open to allow the pilot to let the air out of the inflated balloon. This makes the balloon descend. There are also many ropes that attach to the basket. The basket exterior feels like a woven straw basket, but it is made from a durable material. It has a metal frame and an area for the propane fuel tanks. The heater is positioned just above head level of the pilot and passengers.

After the balloon was carefully laid on the ground, the pilot walked around to check for holes, rips, or tears in the envelope. We then helped him unload a small fan off the truck. This was a fan that had a small airplane type of propeller on it. It would be used to cold-inflate the balloon envelope. Cold inflation is needed to get air into the balloon to get it to take shape. Once the fan was started, it was my job to hold open the lower end of the balloon so that the air could go inside. I must admit this was quite exciting and educational.

Once the balloon was about half-inflated with the cold inflation, the pilot turned the burner to the side and pulled the ignition rope. Wow! The flame sounds like a fire-breathing dragon as it shoots out from the burner. You can feel the heat from several feet away. My job became very important, as I had to make sure the lower end of the balloon did not get in the way of the flame. I have since talked to many people who have seen this happen. For some reason, someone would lower the envelope bottom too much and it would catch on fire.

As the warm air enters the balloon and fills it with hot air, the balloon begins to take shape and to rise up from its sideways position. Then, in a glorious moment, the balloon envelope slowly lifts and stands upright. The basket is tethered to the ground so it will not take flight. We were then instructed to get inside the basket and get ready to take off. Once we were aboard we waited for a signal from the race director. As soon as the ground crew let go of the tether ropes, I could feel the balloon beginning to rise.

It was not a fast, jerky ascent but rather a slow, gentle ascent. It felt much like being on an elevator. However, it was so exciting as the crowds from the festival were cheering for all the balloons as they lifted off. As the balloon ascended higher and higher, the cheers from the crowd began fading into the distance. All I could think of was the scene in Wizard of Oz where Dorothy was leaving the Emerald City. The crowd sounded like the Munchkins telling us good-bye.

Once we were in the air, Ron fired off the burner. Whooooosh! The flame shoots high up into the inside of the balloon envelope. This warm air causes the balloon to gain altitude. In fact, Ron explained, the only control of the balloon is up and down. "We are pretty much at the mercy of the wind," he said. He could, however, raise and lower the balloon to find certain wind patterns. Much like multi-layers of wind currents, some altitudes are better than others for the speed of the balloon.

As several balloons lifted off with us, we were in a game called "The Hare and The Hound." A chase balloon, the hare, had lifted off many minutes before all the other balloons (the hounds). The chase balloon would fly for about a half-hour and then land. It would then spread out a huge bulls-eye type of target. The idea of the game was to fly as close as you could to the target and drop a weighted marker. Whoever tossed their marker closest to the bulls-eye would win a very nice prize.

It is interesting to note that the chase balloon was a "specially shaped balloon." It looked like a giant Pepsi can. These types of balloons are becoming very popular and are being built in some very unusual shapes. There are animal balloons, cars, houses, animated characters—just about any idea you have can be made into a hot air balloon. To us, we were in our own special balloon. Ron described the color of his balloon envelope and it sounded like a giant Easter Egg. It had colors of red, yellow, green, and orange arranged in horizontal stripes.

The ride was going great and it was very smooth. Soon we were coming up on the bulls-eye target that was laid out on the ground. We were quite a way off to the side as we neared the target. Ron leaned over the side of the basket and began to twirl the weighted marker. At the right time, he let go of the marker and it fell down to the target. Ron had hit one of the rings on the target but had missed the bulls-eye. He did notice that there was a marker on the bulls-eye from one of the other balloons. He was not discouraged, as he knew that this was a game of luck. Some of the balloons were miles away from the target and had no chance at all of getting their marker close.

As soon as we passed the target, it seemed that some of the balloons were landing. The wind was picking up and some of the balloons were having trouble landing. There were a couple that had landed, and then were pulled several yards on the ground. A few were actually dragged into a fence. Ron decided we would attempt to make a landing and started to descend. We were moving very fast. Too fast. Before we could pull up, Ron noticed a high point on the ground. He knew we were going to hit it and told us to kneel down in the bottom of the basket. I suppose this is something like the "crash landing" position used in airplanes. Ron was standing and firing off the burner in an attempt to get the balloon to rise. Then we hit the ground. Boom! It was much like being in a minor car accident. It was a sudden crash and then we were in the air again. Ron asked if everyone was OK. As James Bond would say, "We were shaken, not stirred." In fact, it was quite like an amusement park ride; only now the wind was picking up and it was going to be difficult to land the balloon.

Ron called the chase truck and alerted them to our situation. He decided we would continue to fly until a suitable landing area could be found. In doing this, our one-hour flight turned into a two-hour flight. There were no other balloons around us. They had all landed. We all knew that in time we would have to land. We only had a little fuel left. However, the wind had picked up even more and we were moving pretty fast.

Then Ron told us that we were almost out of fuel and were going to have to land. Up ahead was a field, and we started to descend a little. Then a gust of wind pushed us and it was too dangerous to land.

Ron ignited the burners again and we started to climb. And then the burner stopped. We were out of fuel. That was not the immediate problem, but the giant oak trees that we were now flying toward were.

Ron told us to assume our crash positions at the bottom of the basket. Everything got quiet. And in a matter of seconds we hit the trees. We hit the trees very hard. The basket was tilted almost sideways. The branches of the trees were coming into the basket. I heard Ron yell something, but everything was happening so quickly. Ron had tried to push the balloon away from the tree and got his hand caught between the basket frame and a huge tree branch. It tore open his hand. It was also tearing a hole in the balloon.

The strong wind had actually pulled us through the trees. Ron told us to stay in our crash positions, because as soon as we cleared the trees, he was going to dump the air in the envelope. This meant that whatever was on the other side of the trees, was where we were going to land. And we were going to land hard.

I felt the balloon going down very fast. We were still on our side. The basket was on its side and being pulled along the ground. It was kind of like being in a washing machine with six other people. We were getting tossed around and we also had the dirt from the ground coming into the basket. We were plowing up the dirt as the basket skidded across the ground.

Finally the balloon stopped moving for a second, but Ron told us not to get out just yet as the wind could actually pick up the balloon again. I don't know if I really heard this or was just so glad to be on the ground that I just jumped out of the basket. I then pulled Ron out. Immediately he ran up and started flattening out the balloon envelope so that the wind would not catch it. The others started making their way out of the basket. We all had dirt, leaves, and tree branches on us.

I then attended to Ron and put a pressure bandage (actually a torn t-shirt) on his bleeding hand. I had known my first-aid training would come in handy one day. I even made a handy sling out of the rest of the t-shirt so he wouldn't be moving his arm around too much. Everyone else was OK. However, the balloon was not. When we hit the trees, it tore three panels out of the balloon. Ron was philosophical. "I can get the balloon patched up. I'm just really happy none of you were hurt."

The chase truck had seen us hit the trees and was trying to get into the field where we landed. When they finally found an opening in the fence, we were already in the process of folding up the envelope. Once the truck pulled up, we put the envelope on the back of the truck and then we lifted up the basket on to the truck bed. Soon, we were on our way back to the festival. The chase crew had called another truck that was also following along with our flight. It was decided that Ron would be taken to the emergency room by the other chase truck and we would take the balloon back to the festival grounds.

Ron needed 10 stitches in his hand. He then met us back at the festival grounds. He joined us in our celebration of our quite exciting hot air balloon adventure. It is something that I can't forget, and something I look back on with a sense of amazement. Although our gentle giant was not so gentle at the end, I only think of the beauty of the experience.

As the "gentle giants" lift off, there is magic in the air. This mass ascension was in Waterloo, Iowa. There were about 60 balloons taking off at the same time.

Chapter 14

"The sea is dangerous and its storms terrible, but these obstacles have never been sufficient reason to remain ashore...unlike the mediocre, intrepid spirits seek victory over those things that seem impossible...it is with an iron will that they embark on the most daring of all endeavors...to meet the shadowy future without fear and conquer the unknown."

—Ferdinand Magellan

Sea Kayaking and Hobie Cats

I love the ocean. It stirs my soul. The rhythm of the sea is hypnotic. The sound of the waves crashing against the shore is pure magic. The creatures of the sea are so interesting. I could, and have, sat on a beach for hours listening to the birds, the waves, and the sounds of nature in all her splendor. I can still remember what the ocean looked like with its many colors of green and blue punctuated by the white of the waves. As I sit here and type this, it is easy to drift to that far away tropical island and enjoy the majesty of the ocean.

Sea kayaking lets a person experience the ocean. I don't mean just by paddling over it. I mean by really being in it. You experience the "feel" of the ocean. Maybe because I am blind I feel it more. It is as if I am one with the ocean—each wave is a different experience. I do love it so.

One of my first experiences with sea kayaking was in Key Largo, Florida. My good friend Roger Kyler and I were there for a scuba diving trip. One day he suggested we rent a couple of kayaks. He was concerned for my safety, as we would be getting far out into the ocean. While there are many several styles and types of kayaks, we would be using the one-person, one-piece kayak. This is not like the enclosed-bow type of kayaks used by the Eskimos. As you are riding high, the kayak is somewhat top-heavy. and the potential for it to tip over is very much a reality. With this in mind, Roger suggested we stay in very shallow water at first to see if I could manage the kayak.

I felt very comfortable right from the start. Roger started beside me and would talk to me so I knew where he was. He told me how to use the paddle for control and maximum efficiency. A kayak paddle has a paddle on each side. The idea is to paddle once on the left and then immediately paddle on the right. By keeping even strokes, this technique propels you forward in a straight direction. It is also possible to hold the paddle down in the water to turn abruptly.

Once I got the hang of it, Roger went directly in front of me. He would talk as he paddled, and I would follow him by about ten feet. He then said we were going to go down to the waterways that were lined with mangroves. Roger did this for a purpose. The mangroves sheltered us from the waves and wind, and it would be easier to handle the kayaks under these conditions. Rog wanted me to feel very confident before we headed for the open sea.

The mangroves have their own special magic. In many of the narrow waterways you can actually feel the branches touch you. You can hear the fish sometimes jumping out of the water as well as the different sounds of the many birds that inhabit this area. The kayaks are well-suited to explore these areas. Their slim silhouettes glide easily through the narrow passages that lead from one mangrove area to another.

After about an hour in the mangroves, Roger said it was time to make it to the open ocean. I followed behind him through the mangroves and out and around the sheltered harbor. Soon I could feel the undulation of the waves increase in frequency and intensity. At times a wave would come up over the front of the kayak. At first this startled me, but I soon learned to expect that on occasion. It was much like a slap in the face and it got my attention that this could turn into a dangerous situation in a very short time. If the kayak were to turn sideways, it could be flipped over very easily. Even though we had on life jackets, the huge waves would make for a difficult situation.

Once we were well out to sea, the waves began a slow, rolling motion. I found this to be very relaxing. The kayak would drop down with the wave and it would feel very much like an elevator that goes down very quickly. Then it would come up and over the crest of the wave. This is where it is really important to always be going directly into the wave. Once again I was amazed at the vastness and sheer power of the ocean. I could have stayed out there forever. There I was, in the Atlantic Ocean, riding rhythmically up and down on the waves. I put it in perspective when I thought about how I was in a very small boat in one of the world's great oceans. I thought of how the planet Earth is very much like that in the galaxy. I not only learned a lot about kayaking that day, but I learned about myself. Our bodies are like kayaks and the waves are like days. In the big picture, our lives may seem insignificant compared to the lives of billions of people, but each new wave brings a new experience.

My next experience with kayaks was on a different ocean and with a different type of kayak. I was in Puerto Vallarta, Mexico, enjoying the tropical breezes coming off the Pacific Ocean. My friend Rick Bennett suggested we try a two-person kayak. Rick is an accomplished sailor, and in fact is a kindred spirit when it comes to the ocean. It was decided that I would sit in the front position so Rick would be able to steer the kayak.

The sea was very rough. The waves were crashing against the shore. Getting through the surf would be difficult due to the intensity of the waves. Rick told me it was very important that we not get sideways. If we happened to turn sideways into the waves, we would get swamped. There was a very real possibility of physical danger if we were overturned.

I sat down in the front seat and Rick pushed us off. Wham! I was hit immediately by a wave. It came up over the front of the kayak and hit me right in the face. It startled me. It was much like being in a car accident where you are thrown violently back in your seat. I thought I was going to be knocked out of the kayak. The wave almost knocked the paddle out of my hands. I now knew what Rick had meant when he talked about us turning sideways. The kayak would be swallowed by a huge wave.

Wham! Before I could say anything to Rick, I was hit by another wave. It hit me with even a greater impact than the first wave. I was trying to concentrate on paddling straight toward the waves. I couldn't see when the waves were going to come up over the boat, and this was leading to some anxiety on my part. Wham! Another wave. I had my mouth open and swallowed some seawater. This is not a pleasant experience. Wham! Another wave. I now thought that one of the waves might actually push the kayak end over end. Wham! Another wave. I didn't know how much more of this I could handle because I couldn't see where the waves were breaking. Then it became calm.

We had made it through the surf. It was amazing the difference the rough surf had made. We were now in open water. Rick and I discussed the surf and he said he was happy to get through it—he knew I was. However, we were now on our way to open sea. We were paddling into the sun and it felt good on my face. We settled in at a very relaxing pace. We paddled for a long time and then we hit some giant swells. The kayak would roll with the ocean, as we would rise high and then immediately go down low. Rick estimated the swells at eight to 10 feet. We were so far out into the ocean that people had lost sight of us. They would tell us later that sometimes they could see us as a tiny dot on the horizon. Of course when the swells took us down, there was no sight of us from shore. Once again it gives you a real sense of perspective on the might of the ocean.

After a few hours, Rick said that we should probably head back. We had come a long way. It would be easier going back as the waves were helping us. You could feel the giant swells push the kayak. It was so relaxing and peaceful.

Rick told me what we needed to do to get to the shore. We would let the waves do the work. However, it was critical that we keep the kayak headed straight for the beach. It could be disastrous if we got turned sideways. I could hear the waves crashing up ahead. "Here we go!" yelled Rick. A wave propelled us ahead at a fast rate of speed. Then the frequency of the waves began to pick up. Needless to say, coming in to the beach was a lot faster than going out through the surf. Soon I heard the bottom of the kayak scrape the sand. We had made it back from our great adventure.

Sometimes, when I am challenged by something, I think about that particular day of sea kayaking. To make it to open water, you have to just keep paddling, and eventually you will make it. I suppose life is like that sometimes. We are all faced with tough situations and rough seas. It is important to keep paddling—don't give up—and you will make it through.

It was also on the Puerto Vallarta trip that we decided to charter a 45-foot sailboat. A sailboat upon the ocean is poetry in motion. The marriage of the wind and the ocean is enchanting. Graceful and sleek, a sailboat is understated serenity. It glides over the water, creating magic with its wake.

Our boat was named the *Naui*. We boarded, and were introduced to the crew. Captain Alfredo had been sailing for years and personally greeted everyone while helping them board. Nacho and Chavez would make up the rest of the crew. Nacho was like a first mate, deck hand, social director, bartender, and storyteller all combined into one colorful character. He would talk to everyone and make sure their needs were being met. Chavez stayed mainly in the galley (kitchen).

We made our way through the Nuevo Harbor by motor. We passed all types of vessels, everything from small fishing boats to huge cruise ships. It wasn't long until we were out of the harbor and in the Bay of Banderas. Our route would take us from one side of the opening of this huge bay to the other. The sea was very smooth. In fact, it seemed to be more like a lake than an ocean. I began the trip by sitting on the forward deck of the boat. It was a beautiful day for sailing. There was a soft tropical breeze, and I could feel the warmth of the sun.

We hadn't been out to sea long when one of the most magical events occurred. Suddenly, as if on command, several porpoises appeared. They would leap out of the water as if they were performing. At one time three of the delightful creatures leaped from the water and went high into the air. I went to the back of the boat and could actually hear the porpoises as they splashed the water after they jumped. Our new "friends" would stay with us for a long time and it was a delight to have them along.

Captain Alfredo then turned the motor off and had the crew put up the huge sails. It wasn't long before the sails caught the wind and we were under full sail. It is a great feeling to be on a sailboat such as this when the sails are operating at full capacity. I could hear the creaking of the mast as it caught the wind. I could feel the boat gently leaning to one side as the wind shifted. I could sense the motion as the boat glided along the water.

Captain Alfredo then asked me if I wanted to take the wheel. At first I was hesitant because I had never been on a sailboat such as this. I was apprehensive, but Captain Al insisted. It is quite the feeling to take the wheel of a sailboat of this size. I could immediately feel the tension on the wheel and the response of the sail to the wheel. At first Captain Al was right beside me, guiding my every movement. After a while though, he decided to do some fishing off the side of the boat. So there I was, behind the wheel of a 45-footer making its way through the great Pacific.

In a few hours we were at the other side of the bay. We had the option of swimming to the shore or remaining on the boat. Most everyone on board chose to swim to shore. Nacho warned us to be very careful, as there were hundreds of jellyfish near the rocks near shore. These creatures can cause a very painful wound if stepped on or handled carelessly. As I could not see where I was going, I stayed with the other swimmers to avoid an encounter with the jellyfish. The swim was refreshing, but tiring. It was an even harder swim to get back to the boat, as we had to swim against the surf.

Once aboard the boat, we had lunch and then were ready to set sail for our return trip. Captain Alfredo let me take the wheel for most of the trip back to the harbor. I love sailing. I have had many people ask me, "Does it bother you that you can't see the beauty of the ocean?" No, the ocean does not belong to the eyes of the sighted. In fact, the ocean should be "experienced" by many senses. I sometimes think the sighted are left out by their own choice.

> *"To see the sea is not being fully immersed by the ocean. It has to be experienced from within."*
> —*Gary Haun*

While sailing on a 45-foot sailboat is indeed a pleasure, it differs greatly from the exhilaration of a Hobie Cat. A Hobie Cat is a catamaran sailboat that is pure adventure. They can be anywhere from 14 to 18 feet long. They look like two pontoons with a trampoline stretched in between. Most have a huge colorful main sail and a smaller jib sail just ahead of the foremast. They are very light, and this is one of the reasons they are very fast on the water.

Once again I would team up with Rick Bennett to experience a Hobie at its best. First of all, rigging the sail to get it ready for sailing is quite an experience. The mast has to be pushed up while the other person secures it. The lines have to be laid out very methodically or the process has to be repeated. This could prove frustrating for the beginning sailor. Once the boat is in the water, the main sail is then raised. Mother Nature supplies the power. When the wind hits the sail, you had better hold on.

A Hobie glides very fast over the water. At a certain speed it will start to make a humming noise. I compare it to the sound made by a sewing machine. The sailboat will also start rising up on one side. If something isn't done to stop this, it is quite possible that the boat will capsize. This can be prevented by "dumping the sail" or basically letting the wind out of the sail. However, it is quite exciting to be sailing "on the edge" like this.

A Hobie is built so that you sit down on the trampoline part of the boat. In fact, you are sitting only about one to two feet above the surface of the water. It is quite easy to hold your hand over the side and touch the water. Steering is accomplished by a tiller arm that is connected to the rudders. This enables you to capture the maximum effectiveness of the wind. Rick has let me steer the boat on several occasions, and I am still fascinated by the operation of the sails. It is sometimes possible to go as fast or even faster against the wind than sailing with the wind. I thought this was quite impossible until I began sailing. The process of tacking, or sailing at a diagonal, also allows the boat to move when there is hardly any wind at all.

I wish people could "see" sailing from my perspective—the sound of the wake, the sound of the sails as they catch the wind, the feel of excitement as the boat picks up speed, the feel of control as you steer such a sailboat—sailing is so much more than a visual experience. It is a matter of connecting with the elements.

Gary Haun

Balance is very important in sea kayaking. After Roger and I left the relative safety of the mangroves, we headed out to the open waters of the Atlantic Ocean. (Key Largo, Florida)

Chapter 15

"The race goes not always to the swift...but to those who keep on running."

10ks and Marathons

I was introduced to running while in Marine Corps boot camp. It seemed as if we ran every day, usually three to five miles, and sometimes longer distances. We ran in combat boots and would sometimes run with a field pack and an M-14 rifle at port arms. Within about a week, I developed heel contusions. My heels on both feet actually turned jet black. I didn't want to report this to the DIs because they would ridicule anyone who reported for sick bay detail. The drill instructors made it perfectly clear that only "non-hackers" went to sick bay.

I began to run on my toes. If I landed on my heels I would have excruciating pain. I also took a pair of shower shoes and cut off the heel. I placed this rubber heel in my boots so that my heel would have some cushion. It was a primitive orthotic device but it worked—for a while. One morning I scrambled out of the rack at reveille and came down hard on my heels. The pain was indescribable. It felt as if I were standing on a sharp knife. I couldn't walk at all without rising up on my tiptoes. I knew I had to report to the DIs.

Surprisingly, the duty DI sent me to sick bay without the usual "sick bay commando" send-off. He had looked at my feet and could see what the problem was. He knew I was in tremendous pain. I spent my time in sick bay soaking my feet in a whirlpool. After a couple of days the swelling and charcoal black color was gone. My heels were still tender, but I was able to put some weight on them. When I put my shower shoe orthotics in, I was ready to go back to my platoon. My feet still hurt when I ran, but I was able to get through it. I eventually got conditioned to the boots, and as a Marine, would get conditioned to run many, many miles.

Once I got to my regular duty station, I would still have to run. At that time, all Marines had to run as part of the PFT (Physical Fitness Test). All Marines were required to pass the PFT. In order to do so, it meant that the unit you were assigned to would conduct regular training runs to stay in shape to pass the PFT. In today's Marine Corps, running is still a main part of boot camp and the PFT.

After I lost my eyesight and was retired from the Corps, I thought I would never run again. After all, I had trouble getting around with a cane and still would often walk into obstacles. I would always walk rather slowly. I figured if I was going to walk into an obstacle, I would rather hit it at a slow pace.

In 1984 my next door neighbor Pedro Lara asked me if I would like to go running. I told him that I had not run for several years. The truth was that I was a bit uncertain how to do it. My mobility with a cane was good, but running would mean moving fast without a cane. I shared my concerns with Pedro, and he said we could run very slowly while I held on to his arm. I was still apprehensive at first but thought I would like to try it.

We went to the local YMCA and began experimenting with the arm-holding technique. It felt awkward at first but my confidence was growing. We started by going around the track once very slowly. Then we would stop and Pedro would ask how I was doing. After a few weeks, we worked up to a quarter of a mile. We also tried some alternative running methods. One method was for me to hold on to a short piece of rope that was looped around Pedro's arm. While this actually worked very well, it became a problem when we picked up the pace. It threw us both off our stride. Another method was to hold on to a piece of wood that was much like a broomstick. Once again, this worked out fine at a slow pace, but was very difficult to run with at a fast pace.

Once I was comfortable running inside, Pedro suggested we move to the outside track. Once again I was apprehensive. It is hard to explain, but it is like the fear of the unknown. Most blind people move slowly for a reason. It's a matter of simple physics. It hurts less when you bump into something at a slow speed. For me, there was also a mental block of the "tree syndrome." This is thinking I would run head-on into a tree. This did not appeal to me. However, as with most of the adventures I have undertaken, it is a matter of trust. I knew I had to trust Pedro to keep me from "the tree" and any other obstacles.

Once again I shared my concerns with Pedro and we would increase the pace only when I was comfortable. It was also at this time that Pedro introduced me to his friend Dennis Harezlak. Dennis, like Pedro, was an elementary school principal. Personally, I think this is one of the reasons why they ran so well with me. They both have an extreme amount of patience, insight, and understanding. As educators, they understood that this was a learning process for me.

We began running as a team. Pedro on the left and Dennis on the right. This would be a breakthrough in my confidence level. Eventually I dropped the technique of holding on to someone's arm. This enabled me to move both my arms freely, and that meant running faster.

After we worked our way up to three miles, we decided to enter a local fun run. The fun run was in Monroe, Wisconsin, and it was sponsored by a local brewery. This meant free beer at the end of the race. The free beer was a motivational factor at the time. I was apprehensive about entering races. The problem was that I was uncomfortable in crowds, especially when the crowd was running. I knew Pedro and Dennis would keep me out of trouble, but I still had a mental block about running into other runners.

The race was on a brisk November morning. As we were stretching to prepare for the race, it began to sleet. The icy rain soon covered the streets where the race was to take place. I had trouble walking and would slide with every other step. I became very worried about falling. I told Pedro and Dennis to run the race without me. However, they would have no part of this. "We are a team," said Pedro. Dennis added, "We have trained running together, and we will do this race together." And that was that. There is something to be said for having great running partners. They give you confidence and reassurance in your abilities. It was decided that we would start the race by walking, and that I would hold on to the arms of my running partners. We also lined up behind the other runners so we wouldn't have to deal with all the people.

It is exciting when the starting gun goes off. There is a sense of anticipation. We started moving very slowly. Pedro and Dennis were holding me so I would not fall. After about a quarter of a mile, I was actually finding my balance point and becoming more confident of running on the ice-covered road. A sense of achievement came over me. I was so shook up before the race, and now I was actually enjoying this. I felt I was part of something. I felt good. It is times like these that you don't think about being blind, as you are too busy thinking about the immediate situation. I was so happy that I could run in this type of weather as it meant that I could also run in snow. Winter running is a fact of life for runners in Northern Illinois.

We finished the race as we had started. Pedro and Dennis were on both sides of me as we crossed the finish line. Our race time was never an issue in this particular race. Our goal was to finish, and finish we did. It was this race that gave me confidence in my running ability. With Pedro and Dennis, I would run several 10ks (ten kilometers - 6.2 miles). We would increase our weekly mileage and eventually do a seven-mile event and a ten-mile race. Then we decided upon doing a half-marathon (13.1 miles).

Training for the half-marathon is very demanding. It is important that you include some long distance runs in your weekly training. This meant getting up at five o'clock in the morning to begin running. The reason for this is that it keeps you from having to run in the hottest part of the day. Dehydration is very much a concern on any running program, but especially on long-distance running. Our long-distance runs were usually nine to eleven miles. Just before we ran the race we actually ran a 13-mile run. We were ready.

Training is the key to successful running. The half-marathon went very well. By this time I was able to let go of the arms of my running partners. This became an important element in long-distance races— as it sometimes interfered with the running style of my partner. I would start the race by touching the arm of my partner and then let go once the crowd of runners thinned out. Out on the course, Dennis would run up ahead of me to make a way for me to pass other runners. I also wore a running jersey that had "Blind Runner" printed on front and back. This would let other runners know that I might make an erratic turn or suddenly stop.

After our very successful half-marathon we decided we would train for a full marathon (26.2 miles). We would begin our long runs early on Saturday mornings. It was a slow progression from 10-mile runs to 20-mile runs. We decided we would run a 24-miler a few weeks before the marathon. All of our training runs went very well. We all stayed injury-free. There was the usual soreness in the knees, calves, and lower back, but nothing serious. We were ready.

On October 19th, 1986, we lined up with the crowd to start the Rock River Marathon. The starting gun was fired and we took off. Once again I was holding the arm of both Pedro and Dennis until I was comfortable running on my own. The first five miles were pretty easy. When I came into the sixth mile, my support team joined in. My friend Paul Nelson was on a bicycle and would ride beside me until the finish of the race. We made it to the 10th mile feeling great. We were running at about a nine-minute mile, just as we had planned to do. Pedro and Dennis were running great and were not even breathing hard. When we crossed the 16th mile I was beginning to slow down a little. When we crossed the 19th mile marker—I hit "The Wall."

"The Wall" is an imaginary territory that many long-distance runners have to deal with. Some stop running completely. Some start walking and eventually stop and rest. Some try to tough it out to the finish line. I was in some pain, but knew I wanted to finish. I told Pedro and Dennis to go ahead and finish without me. They were running well and I did not want to hold them back. We had discussed this situation before the race, and it was agreed that if one of us could not finish, that the others would go on. Besides, I had Paul on the bike next to me. Also, at the 20-mile marker, my friend Mike DeDoncker would join me for the last six miles of the race.

By the time Mike had joined me, I was feeling terrible. I felt completely exhausted. I can't say that there was a time when I wanted to quit, but there were several times where I questioned the purpose of going on. I made it to the 23-mile mark. Only three more miles to go. I was now in severe pain. My feet hurt. My legs hurt. My back hurt. Why was I punishing myself like this? 24 miles…my mind was telling my body that I could make it to the finish. My body was telling my mind that it hurt. 25 miles…I truly knew what it meant to hit "The Wall," but now it felt like I was pulling "The Wall" with me. I started to think about my childhood, and then it struck me that this sometimes happens to people who are close to death. Then Mike snapped me out of my negative mental state by saying, "One more mile. C'mon, you're gonna make it!"

People were lined up the last mile to cheer me on. I actually picked up the pace going toward the finish line. The crowd was clapping their hands as I ran across the finish line. My time was 4:59:03. Our goal was to run the marathon in less than five hours. Pedro and Dennis were the first to shake my hand. I thanked everyone who had helped me. I couldn't have done it without them. I then sat down on a curb and rested. I was so glad to be done. At the time, there was no sense of accomplishment. I was still sore all over. My body ached from my head to my toes. I went home, lay down, and took some aspirin. It was difficult for me to walk for the next day or so. Walking up and down stairs was the worst. However, the following Monday I would walk up the stairs at Rockford's City Hall. The mayor wanted to give me a certificate for being the first blind person to finish the Rockford Marathon.

After running the marathon, I met some new running partners. Terri Gray, Sandy Bass, Jan Foust, Sue Anderson, and Char Sackmaster all ran at the same time I was at the YMCA. My wife, Donna, approached Terri and asked if any of them would run with me. Donna ran much too fast for me and it would only slow her down to run my pace. And so it came to be that I would wind up running with five of the nicest people in the world. We would run three to five times a week. It was so nice to run with this group, as it was relaxed running. Sue would often bring her dog along. Jan and I had gone to junior high school together and would talk about that. It was a good feeling to run with so many positive people.

The following year, Terri Gray said that she would like to do a marathon. I still had bad memories about the first marathon, but I told Terri I would train with her. We designed a training plan and all our training runs were great (we once ran twenty miles at an eight-minute pace). However, once again, I hit the wall at 19 miles!

Terri could have run the marathon in less than four hours. She was light on her feet even at the end of the race. However, she stuck with me to the finish line. We finished in 4:35:04.

I joined the Rockford Road Runners in 1988. My introduction to this local running club was through Ray Treadway. Ray was in his late 70s and was still running. Ray also introduced me to the "Monster Run." This is a seven-mile course that is known for its steep hills. I was always amazed at Ray, as he would finish the Monster and still want to do a couple more miles. Ray is certainly an inspiration to all who aspire to be young at heart.

Of all the races I have entered, the Survival Run was the most challenging. The Survival Run is a 10k race through the wilderness. It consists of running through a thick forest, through shallow creeks, through mud pits, and crawling up steep hills. When everyone finishes, they are covered with mud and dirt. Most run in old running shoes so they can throw them away at the end of the race. Just before you finish the race you have to deal with "The Mountain," which is a slippery, 308-foot steep hill.

In this particular race, our strategy was different. Mike DeDoncker would run up ahead of us and yell back, telling me what to expect. I held the arm of either Paul Nelson or Pedro throughout the race. When I got to "The Mountain," I was on my own to crawl up the hill. I would feel for a tree branch to hold on to and then pull up. At one point in the race, we had to run through a creek. What no one knew was that the crossing was just wide enough for one runner to cross. I was holding on to Pedro's arm and we started to cross. Pedro was on the crossing but I was not. As I moved forward I stepped into a hole—a deep hole. Mike would say later, "I looked back and all I saw of Gary was his hat." I went in over my head. Pedro pulled me out and we kept running. Later we all had a good laugh about this. However, I was not amused at that moment. There were also trees that were lying across the path. We would stop, and Paul would tell me where to lift and place my feet to get over the tree. At times I found this to be very frustrating, but we would go about it in a very methodical way. We finished the race in 1:04, but honestly, this is a race that we were happy just to finish.

One of the highlights of my running experiences was running with my friend Mike DeDoncker. Mike is a sports writer for the *Rockford Register Star* newspaper, and is involved in many different sports. Mike had helped me during the last six miles of my first marathon. We began by doing several training runs together. We would eventually run several 10ks, half-marathons, trail runs, and various other races together. However one race was particularly interesting.

Mike is an intense person. He gives everything 110 percent. One of our first races together was a local 10k. It was a beautiful day and we prepared for the race as we had planned. We stretched and ran a short while to warm up. We lined up for the race and I was holding Mike's arm to get around in the crowd of runners. When the gun went off, we started running right away. This was unusual as in most of the races, it took a while for the crowd to thin out. As soon as we were in the open, I let go of Mike's arm. I could tell we were running fast—very fast. I think the term "moving like greased lightning" would describe this first mile very well. We were really moving. It was the only mile I have ever run without talking. Fact is, I couldn't. The only words Mike was saying were, "Pass left" or "Pass right." We were passing people as if they were walking. While it is not unusual to pass people near the end of a race, it was very unusual to be passing people in the first mile.

We were running so fast that I was breathing like a Kentucky racehorse, but I felt good. I didn't have any side aches like many runners get while running at a pace such as this. We passed more people. I was running so fast that I outran my "blind man running into a big tree" problem. As I mentioned before, I had (and sometimes still have) a mental block that would slow me down as I was so afraid of running into something. However, in this first mile, I was just running hard and was only thinking about running. I could hear the first-mile timekeeper calling off the time as runners passed by. As Mike and I passed by he yelled 5:16. This would be the fastest mile I had ever run in my life!

Mike and I were in a state of shock. It was almost scary. First of all, I thought that I was incapable of running that fast. Secondly, I had become accustomed to running at an eight- to nine-minute-per-mile pace. This was incredible. Then at about the same moment, it dawned on us that we were in a 10k race. We still had five miles to go. Needless to say, we slowed down the pace. In fact, we had to walk a bit at the end. However, it was a banner day. One I will never forget.

In 1989 I began doing biathlons. This would usually consist of a two-mile run, followed immediately by a 15-mile bike ride, and then another two-mile run. My friend Paul Nelson had done several of these types of races, and I became interested in them. With that, I bought a tandem (a bicycle built for two) racing bike. Of course Paul would steer and I would sit in the back position. We practiced on the bike to get familiar with it. We would learn how to lean into corners together and when to set our feet down when we stopped. I must admit that I really enjoyed biking. The tandem was fun, and while it was tough to go up a hill, it was like a heat-seeking missile coming down a hill.

The following year I entered my first triathlon. The triathlon would consist a quarter-mile swim, a 15-mile bike ride, and a three-mile trail run. I would team up for this event with Pedro Lara, as he had competed in several triathlons and would also be able to do all three events with me. I was experienced in running and biking from doing the biathlons. However, I was new to swimming. I began a lap-training program at the YMCA until I was ready to practice swimming with Pedro. We began swimming the actual course in the lake where the triathlon was to be held.

I was having trouble staying on course. Unlike running, where I could hold on to someone's arm, I had a habit of swimming at an angle. Pedro suggested bringing in a swimming coach to help solve the problem. Dana Replogle had competed in several triathlons, and was more than willing to help us out. She came out to the lake to see how we were swimming. She then worked with me to get me swimming like a lifeguard. I would swim with my head out of the water so that I could listen to what was going on. Also, I would actually touch Pedro with every third or fourth stroke I took. This method worked very well, and the swim segment of the triathlon went very well.

It was also during this time that I met Debi Ward. She had just gotten in to running. Her fiancé (now husband), John Ellis, was quite an accomplished runner, but ran much faster and farther than Debi wanted to run. I remember when we first began to run. We started doing a half-mile and gradually progressed to three miles. We then began to work on speed, and also eventually would do some long-distance runs. Debi progressed rather quickly and soon we were running races together. In 1995 we decided we would train to do a half-marathon.

Debi is such a nice person that it was enjoyable to run with her. She would always feel bad if she had to stop and walk. It also seemed that she was more concerned about me than she was about herself. I think that I was just lucky to have her as a running partner. We trained for a year to do the half-marathon. I must admit that we trained well and we were confident on race day. Debi ran great that day and it turned out to be one of the best half-marathons I have ever run.

The following year I would run the same half-marathon with Nonie Broski. It was amazing that Nonie would be running such a long distance, as she had only been training for less than a year. I knew Nonie would have no trouble with the race because she ran the 10 to 12-mile training runs so well. Once again, all the training paid off and we had a great half-marathon.

Today I still run two to three times a week. My primary running partners are Sandy Bass, Debi Ward, and Terri Gray. They are the best running partners anyone could have. I feel safe when I run with them. This is important to a blind runner. It makes it easier to enjoy the run instead of worrying about what you are going to run into. Oh, by the way, sometimes things just happen. During the years I have been running, I have run into nine trees, two garbage cans, four ducks, two toddlers on Hot Wheels, three bicycles, and a parked car.

I have never won a race. I have never received any trophies or medals for any of the races I have competed in. I don't need any. For me, merely lining up at the starting line is an achievement. No, my trophies and medals are when, at the end of a training run, my running partners say, "Good run, Gary!"

Chapter 16

"Be thou the rainbow in the storms of life; the evening beam that smiles the clouds away and tints tomorrow with prophetic ray."

—Byron

Manatees and Dolphins

Of all God's creatures, the manatee is certainly one of the most interesting. These large marine animals migrate to the warm coastal and river waters of Florida during the winter months. They look like walruses without the tusks, and their faces resemble those of their closest relatives—the elephants. They average about 1,000 pounds, but can grow up to about 1,500 pounds. In days of old, sailors who obviously had been out to sea too long, thought manatees were mermaids. I suspect it was too much ale.

Crystal River on the west coast of Florida is one of the favorite places of the manatees. They like the warm water of the river and come there from the Gulf of Mexico. It is like a winter home for the manatee and also a favorite place for humans to get to know and learn about these magnificent animals. Hopefully, through education and conservation efforts, the manatee population will continue to grow. For many years the existence of the manatees was in doubt. While a manatee can live up to 60 years, many become casualties of boat propellers, pollution, entanglement in fishing lines, and loss of habitat. Also, many become ill because of rapid changes in water temperature.

For many years I was reluctant to go swim with the manatees because I did not want to be part of the problem. That is, I did not want to disturb their environment. I then found out about the education, conservation, and preservation efforts that were being done in association with swimming with the manatees. I contacted American Pro Dive Center and set up a trip to visit with these mystical creatures. I decided that February would be the best time to go, as this is one of the times when there are a large number of manatees in the river.

It was early in the morning when Roger and I met our friends Emmett and Terri Gray at the dive shop. I had told them about this trip and they too, wanted to meet the manatees. After getting sized up for our wetsuits, we sat down for a briefing on what to do and what not to do around the manatees. We then watched and listened to a video describing manatee behavior and conservation efforts to help protect these endangered animals. They are protected under federal law by the Marine Mammal Protection Act and also the Endangered Species Act.

At the boat dock, we boarded a large pontoon boat with about 10 other divers. As we were making our way to the area where the manatees were, we were again briefed on what behavior to expect from the manatees, and more importantly, what our behavior should be. We were told not to bother any mothers with calves and not to make sudden erratic movements, as this would scare off the manatees. We were also told not to push, pull, poke, or jab and definitely not to try to ride one.

Soon the manatees were spotted. A manatee has to surface about every three to five minutes for a breath of air. The rest of the time is spent searching for food, resting, or moving from place to place. The manatees are herbivorous (plant eaters) and eat aquatic plants where they can find them. This was obviously one of their favorite areas because the people were very excited about how many manatees were in this one area.

We entered the water very slowly so as not to disturb the manatees. The water was about four feet deep so there was no need to snorkel or swim to the animals. Basically, while Roger was taking some underwater photos, I was standing still and alone by myself.

Within minutes a huge manatee swam over to me. It was magic. He very gently bumped my leg and then started feeding on the vegetation near my foot. I slowly reached out and touched him. It was an incredible experience. I was so happy.

His skin was rough like a cow's skin, and covered with algae. I stroked him on his back as if I was combing him with my fingers. I strangely felt that he was enjoying this type of attention, and he must have—he stayed with me for about 15 minutes. As I felt around his body, I got an idea of how big he was. Roger told me later that this particular manatee would weigh about 900 pounds and would measure about 10 feet long. I felt his front flippers that he swims with. They have no back legs and have a flat, paddle-shaped tail. I continued to move my hand slowly along his back and I could feel the scars from the manatee's misfortunate encounter with a boat propeller. You can't help but feel sorry for these creatures that would not harm any one.

A meeting with a manatee in his environment surely makes a person concerned about the existence and future of such an animal. In the short time of my contact with this manatee, I could not help but think, "Will he be here tomorrow?" I sure hope so. It is hard to believe that someone would intentionally harm one of these animals. I am glad there are laws to protect them.

After another diver came over to photograph this particular manatee, he slowly moved away. Then when the diver left, this same manatee came back to me and started to feed on the vegetation. It was almost as if the manatee sensed that I was blind and that he knew I could not follow him around. I also believe the slow movements of my hand on his back had a soothing effect on him—almost like a massage. Whatever the reason, I was happy to be here and experience this, and wished that all people could do this. I believe it connects you with the beauty of nature.

After this manatee moved away I started moving toward the other divers. Roger was filming underwater and came up and told me to stop moving. "There are four manatees in a group right in front of you," he said. I could feel them moving around in front of me. Then I heard one come up for air. It is hard to describe what a sound like this means to a blind person. I felt that it was a direct link to understanding these animals. I can still hear that sound when I dream about the manatees.

If the manatee is like a big lovable sheepdog, then the dolphin would be like a lovable puppy. They are so energetic and love to play. The dolphin can speed through the water and then jump high into the air. Like the manatee, the dolphins like to be in contact with humans. They are adorable.

A dolphin is not a fish, but in fact, a mammal. They give live birth and breathe with lungs. Although they have teeth, the dolphins do not use them to chew with, but rather to hold on to their food. They are very intelligent and seem to be able to communicate with one another.

I have always been fascinated by dolphins and interested in their behavior. I decided I would like to learn more about them and contacted a few of the research facilities for more information. Since I was going to Key Largo, Florida, to do some scuba diving, I decided to visit Dolphin Cove Research and Education Center. Dolphin Cove is a marine environment research facility and they also offer dolphin encounter programs.

The staff at Dolphin Cove was very enthusiastic about my visit. I had told them I was blind and they said that several disabled people had participated in their program. It is interesting to note that the dolphins seem able to sense that a person has a disability. I sensed this as I swam with the dolphins. It was as if they knew I could not see, and would gently move around me. I know it sounds strange, but it was as if we were communicating through our thoughts.

After I arrived at the facility, I was introduced to Mary Lycan. She is a specialist in dolphin behavior and would guide me through the entire process. The first thing was an orientation about dolphins—basic anatomy, habitat, behavior, diet, and other information about dolphins was discussed. I really enjoyed this and was amazed at the many things I did not know about dolphins. Mary talked about dolphins with a passion that very well communicates her concern for the welfare of these wonderful animals.

Then our discussion turned to the behavior I could expect from the dolphin and what activities he would do with me. We also discussed what I would be doing when I entered the water. As expected, I was told to move slowly as possible, as quick movements might frighten the dolphin. Mary explained all these things in such a way that I felt very comfortable about what was going to happen.

We then moved to a platform overlooking the cove. As I knelt down with Mary, she took my hand and we gently "tapped" on top of the water. This was a signal for the dolphin to come to the platform. As I mentioned, dolphins are very intelligent, and they have been conditioned to respond to this signal. I suspect that they know they will get a fish treat if they respond.

I then heard the dolphin surface. "Gary, meet Duke," said Mary. "Duke, shake hands with Gary." And then, as I stretched out my hand, I felt the fin of the dolphin. It was pure magic. Moments like this only come around once in a person's life. I felt an electricity of positive feelings by just touching this animal. It was much more than just the touch. It was a connection. I was meeting a new friend. In my dreams I can still feel that first touch.

Duke was a juvenile dolphin, and like most young dolphins, liked to play. It was as if he was trying to show off. He would swim in a circle and then jump high into the air. You could sense he was having fun. I also liked the clicking sound he made. He sounded happy.

Mary then instructed me to slowly enter the water. I sat on the platform and turned as I pushed myself out into the water. I had my wetsuit on so I was buoyant and well out of the water at chest level.

Mary then told me to hold my arms straight out. I felt Duke rise out of the water and slowly move past me. Mary wanted me to get a feel for what Duke looked and felt like. His skin was very smooth. Very different from a manatee or a shark. His dorsal fin was round and smooth. I then felt his tail fin as he went by.

As he was making his circle, Mary told me to lie on my back in a relaxed position. This was quite easy because I had the wetsuit on. As soon as I was on my back, I felt Duke easing toward me and pressing his nose against my feet. All of a sudden, he started pushing me. And like a tugboat, Duke was pushing me around in circles. After doing this several times, he stopped and came around in front of me. It was as if he was making sure I was okay. Wow!

Then Mary told me to put my arms out to my side. She told me that when Duke came up out of the water, I should hold on to his fin. As soon as she said this, Duke eased up beside me. I grabbed on to his dorsal fin and it was as if a ski boat were pulling me. Duke almost jumped out of the water with me hanging on to him. He went speeding around in circles, with me hanging on for dear life. What an incredible experience. Once again, after he stopped and I let go, Duke came around in front of me to see if I was okay.

When Duke was underwater, I could sense him coming toward me from a long way off. Even though Mary had worked with blind people before, she was amazed at how far off I could sense Duke's presence. It is like a magnified kinesthetic perception that worked both ways. He sensed I was blind and adjusted his movements to me, and I had a sense of his movement and presence even when he was more than 100 feet away and underwater.

Just before I was ready to come out of the water, Mary said, "Duke, give Gary a kiss." Slowly, while upright in the water, Duke moved toward me. I could feel his presence and also hear him. He came within about six inches of my face, and then, very gently pushed his face up against my cheek. Magic, pure magic. I will never forget that moment.

Gary Haun

After shaking hands with my new friend, "Duke" the dolphin, he pulled me around the lagoon. Truly a beautiful and lovable animal.

Chapter 17

"Some people are so afraid to die that they never begin to live."

—Henry Van Dyke

Sharks

Admittedly, jumping into the water when you are surrounded by sharks is not for everyone. The usual response is, "You're crazy! You gotta be nuts!" Or, "Do you have a death wish?"

No, quite honestly, I have a life wish. The feeling of a ten-foot shark nudging up against you makes you very aware that you are glad to be alive. It is an electrifying, adrenaline-pumping, and heart-thumping experience. It magnifies and intensifies life. It is much like skydiving—a total sensory overload.

Before I could swim with the sharks, I first had to learn to scuba dive. I contacted the local dive shop and signed up for classes. Although they had never trained a blind person before, they were very enthusiastic and positive about my coming to class. This was very encouraging, because I had been told previously that I could not become a certified diver. In fact, I would have tried scuba diving several years before, but I had so many people tell me that I could not do it. I believed them. This is why I always include this message when I give talks to elementary schools: Do not let others put limitations on your dreams and goals. If you are constantly told that you cannot do something, that your goal is unattainable, that your dream is unrealistic or foolish—you will eventually come to believe this and thus—make those limitations a reality. It is frustrating not to be given a chance to try.

At the beginning of scuba classes, I was introduced to the instructor, Jeff Tobey. And once again I was pleasantly surprised by the positive outlook. Jeff made it perfectly clear that I would be expected to do everything a sighted diver would have to do. That included classroom lectures, written examinations, swimming pool skills, and of course, the open water test. Then Jeff said that we would find methods that would help me accomplish all of these skills. I liked his attitude. It was not one of—there are going to be many problems in doing this—but rather, there are some problems we need to overcome, so let's try to work them out as we progress.

The classroom lectures and written tests were no problem. I took notes with a tape recorder, and I used my reading machine to read the divers manual. I also had a Braille dive table made up. This is used to calculate how much time you need for a surface interval between dives. It is important to know how much excess nitrogen you have in your body. Nitrogen builds up in the body during diving, and too much can lead to DCS (decompression sickness).

I also used many different hand signals during the swimming pool instruction. Along with the standard underwater signals, we also invented some new ones. For example, to let a sighted diver know he had completed a skill successfully, the instructor would make the OK signal—making a circle by touching the index finger to the thumb. Since I could not see this signal, Jeff would shake my hand. If he wanted me to practice clearing water from my mask, he would take my hand and tap it on my mask. We would adapt many signals from rescue divers, as these divers often work in very cloudy water and sometimes zero visibility.

For the open water dive, I purchased a Mares Divemate dive computer. Dive computers can give the diver important data such as depth, dive time, no stop time (time remaining before a decompression stop is needed), surface time, and many other functions. It also gives warnings such as ascent rate and when to make a safety stop. What makes the Divemate perfect for me is that it talks. The computer has an audio mode that speaks all the above information. It will actually tell you to slow down if you are making too fast of an ascent. I suppose this technology was originally designed for cave divers, rescue divers, and underwater welders so that the diver would not have to look at the computer, or for times when the diver would not be able to see the computer due to poor visibility.

I also acquired a Braille compass. I was surprised that the compass worked so well underwater. Today there is a compass that has an audio function that "speaks" the same way as the Divemate. I also used a light probe to read my pressure gauge. I used a watertight bag to put the light probe in, much like the bags that some underwater photographers put their cameras in. I have since found out that there is an audible pressure gauge that is used by divers in underwater welding and maintenance.

Jeff wanted to make sure that I could do all the things that any diver would have to do. He was very thorough and professional. We would practice primary skills such as buoyancy control, removing and replacing equipment, alternate breathing techniques, and many other skills—over and over again. All the training paid off, because by the time I was ready for the open water tests, I was very confident of my abilities. Although the water was very cold (58 degrees), I felt comfortable under water. I passed all my tests and became a certified Open Water Diver. I was so happy.

I have made several dives since my certification. However, I still approach each dive the way I was taught. I check and recheck all my equipment. I dive within my limits and capabilities, and always remember the words "plan your dive, dive your plan." Of course I always remember to make a slow descent (this is to allow the body to equalize to the pressure changes), and to ascend slowly (to avoid DCS—decompression sickness).

The only requirement of my certification is that I must always be with another diver. Personally, even if I had my eyesight, I would want this to be a requirement. I feel it is much safer to have a dive buddy around in case you get into trouble.

I would advise anyone who is thinking about taking up scuba diving to seek out a reputable and professional instructor. I am amazed at how many divers I have talked to who do not know many of the basics—even some who cannot swim!

Nassau, Bahamas: Caribbean Reef Sharks

Stuart Cove's Dive South Ocean is one of the world's best known dive operations, especially for shark diving. It is located on the island of New Providence in the Bahamas, and is about a 25-minute drive from downtown Nassau. Stuart Cove is known internationally for his work with the film industry and his expertise with sharks. He has helped with the underwater sequences involving sharks in such films as *James Bond—Never Say Never Again, For Your Eyes Only, Cocoon, Splash, Flipper,* and many more. He has also been featured in many documentaries about sharks.

I chose Stuart Cove's on a recommendation from the Handicapped Scuba Association, of which I am a member. A group of divers from HSA had recently been on a shark dive at Stuart Cove's. They had a great time and were quite impressed with the operation. I then made arrangements to go do a shark dive.

The staff at Stuart Cove's is so friendly and nice that it takes your mind off the diving itself. But reality sets in when you sign the required waiver stating that you understand that this activity can be hazardous—and you do it at your own risk. It reminded me of signing the forms when I went skydiving.

Roger and I went to the shop four hours before the dive so I could meet with the divemaster. I would be with the divemaster at all times and I wanted to go over all the hand signals we would be using. This is something I do on all my dives.

I was introduced to Alda du Plooy, a young lady who had dived with other blind divers. She was very professional and immediately put me at ease about the dive. We went over the hand signals we would be using and added a new one. Alda would squeeze my wrist three times when a shark was near. This is very important because a sudden, erratic movement might cause the shark to react in an unpleasant way. She also wanted me to squeeze her wrist when I sensed the presence of a shark.

We also discussed the behavior of sharks. It is too bad that many people, especially children, think of all sharks as *"Jaws."* Alda explained that "humans are not on the menu—just remember that we are going into their environment and we must respect that environment." While all sharks are predators, they are not all man-eaters.

We would be making two dives. The first, called "The Runway Wall," goes along the wall of the "Tongue of the Ocean." This is one of the deepest parts of the ocean and goes down to a depth of over 6,000 feet. This would be a "free swim" along the wall to a depth of about 60 feet. We would then swim to a flat, sandy area and sit down to rest before heading back up to the boat. The second dive would be at the "Shark Runway."

This is where all the divers would be assembled in a semi-circle on a flat, sandy area at a depth of about 50 feet. The feeder/divemaster would then bring down a box of chum (cut up fish—shark yummies) and sit in the middle of the group. He would then open the box, spear some chum, and the sharks would come into the area for a snack.

The boat ride to the dive site was an experience in itself. From the time we had arrived on the island, we had strong winds (sometimes gale force) and heavy rain. Although we only had to go out about five miles, the sea was churning with white-capped waves and 15-foot swells. It seemed to me as if we were in a hurricane. My fear was not of the sharks, but in getting on and off the boat in these conditions.

After being given all the last minute instructions about the dive, everyone began donning their wetsuits and scuba gear. There were about 14 divers in our group. After all the divers entered the water, Alda led me to the back of the boat. Just as I was instructed to do, I sat down on the diving platform with my legs hanging over the edge. I then turned and pushed away from the boat and entered the water. The sea was very rough, but within seconds Alda was right beside me. Because of the turbulent conditions, we started our descent immediately. We both grabbed the dive guideline that went to the bottom. We slowly inched our way down the line, remembering to equalize as we descended. Because of the 15-foot swells, we would have to let go of the rope when the boat would rise, so that we would not be violently pulled up with it. Alda handled this situation so well that it never became a problem. When we were about 20 feet down, we left the rope and descended on our own.

It is hard to describe what scuba diving is like for me. I have had so many people say, "Scuba diving is so visual, how can you enjoy it?" First of all, getting off the boat was, for me, a major accomplishment. I was so afraid that the boat might hit me in the face when I entered the water. I was also apprehensive that Alda might have trouble getting to me in the rough water. I was worried that I might have trouble equalizing and that I would have to return to the boat. None of these things came to be—and here I was on the adventure of a lifetime.

The feeling of neutral buoyancy is also an incredible feeling. I imagine that this feeling of weightlessness is something like what astronauts experience in zero gravity. The sound of your bubbles is relaxing. The slow breathing process is very soothing. It's my impression that sighted people often think the visual experience is the only experience in scuba diving. But I often wonder if, by using their vision so much, sighted people might be missing out on the "whole picture."

Within about five minutes of leaving the dive rope, I was bumped on my right shoulder. I thought it was Roger, who was diving with Alda and me. What I did not know was that after entering the water, Roger had a problem with his weight belt and was still on the boat. In the same instant that I was going to wave to "Roger," Alda gave me three quick squeezes on my wrist. We had a new diving partner. Alda would tell me later that a huge Caribbean reef shark had come up behind us and bumped me on the shoulder. This was not that unusual, as the sharks were swimming all along the same wall as we were. While it did not frighten me when Alda squeezed my hand, it immediately brought to my attention that I was just a visitor to the shark's home. I was in their environment and I had better respect it.

We dived along the wall of the "Tongue of the Ocean" to a depth of about 65 feet. The other group of divers went deeper, some to over 100 feet. At the end of the dive, we went to a flat, sandy area and sat on the bottom. This was very relaxing, almost like being on the bottom of a swimming pool. The water was warm, about 78 degrees, and at this depth, there was no turbulence. In fact, it is hard to imagine that on the surface, the sea was so rough.

While we were sitting in this area, we were visited by several sharks. At one time I was boxed in by four sharks. It made for a great picture. The sharks were very close and I could actually feel their presence as they glided by.

Alda gave me the signal that it was now time to make our ascent. We would be swimming to the dive rope that would lead us up to the boat. Once we made it to the rope, we began a nice, slow ascent. We made our required safety stop at 15 feet for three minutes. Once again, we would let the rope slide through our hands, so the boat would not pull us up out of the water. The swells were so huge that if we did not let go of the rope, we would have been pulled up to the surface.

Once we came to the surface, we had to pull ourselves toward the boat. The choppy water made this very difficult, but I finally made it to the boat. Once again I thought I might have trouble getting into the boat in these conditions. But, with the expertise of the boat crew and divemasters, I made it aboard with no problem.

While making our 30-minute surface interval, Alda and I discussed the dive. She told me about the shark bumping me, and that she had been afraid that I might react by quickly reaching out toward the shark. This would have been very dangerous, as sharks react to sudden movements. Or the shark could have confused my hand with a fish and attacked it. She also described the scene when I had the sharks surrounding me.

It was now time for our second dive. Again we were briefed on what to do. Alda and I made our way off the boat and down the rope as we did in our first dive. As soon as we reached the bottom, we were arranged in a semi-circle. Alda knelt beside me, and Roger was on my other side. He had an underwater camera and would be filming the sharks.

Soon the divemaster for the whole group came down with a huge box that contained the chum. He positioned himself in the middle of the group. It was not long before the sharks arrived. It was as if someone had rung the dinner bell. They came in slowly at first, as if they were checking everything out. Then they became more aggressive as the divemaster would open the box and produce a piece of chum. He would spear some chum and hold it up for the sharks to eat.

About twenty Caribbean reef sharks soon surrounded us. At first the males came in. They are smaller but more aggressive than the females. They move very quickly and turn rapidly. After a while the huge females came in. These sharks can be more than ten feet long, and seem to move more slowly than the males. At one point during the dive, a huge female came from behind us and went right in between Alda and me. The shark actually rubbed up against me as it went through. It lightly smacked me in the face with its tail fin. That was an incredible feeling. The rough skin of the shark (much like sandpaper) pulled against my dive suit. Alda knew I was excited as I squeezed her hand three times. She took her free hand and tapped me on the back to acknowledge this event. Even today, when I reflect back on this dive, I can still feel the shark. When I talk to Roger about these dives, we both agree it is surrealistic, almost as if being in a dream.

After about a half-hour of feeding the sharks, it was time to ascend to the boat. I made it up and on to the boat in the same manner as the first dive. The ride back through the rough sea was slow. However, I was feeling great. Some people say, "Why would anyone put themselves in danger like that?" The real danger in life is in feeling sorry for yourself, in not being excited about life, in thinking negatively, and in not living life to its fullest.

> *"Having sharks surround you is not a problem. No, having the dark clouds of despair and negativity surrounding you is much worse."*
> —*Gary Haun*

Gansbaai, South Africa: The Great White Shark

Probably the best known shark is the Great White. Unfortunately, due to movies such as *"Jaws,"* these sharks have been labeled as man-eaters and indiscriminate killers. This is too bad, as many children are afraid to swim in the ocean waters, and equally bad for the sharks who are killed in large numbers out of fear. Only recently have the Great Whites become protected under the endangered species laws of several nations.

One of the largest concentrations of Great Whites is in the waters off the coast of South Africa. In fact, about five-and-a-half nautical miles out from the town of Gansbaai, is an area named "Shark Alley." This channel is between two islands, Dyer Island and Geser Island. On Geser Island there is a colony of over 7,000 cape fur seals. The Great Whites come in to feed on the seals, and these favorable conditions make it one of the best areas in the world to study these sharks.

Since I was going to Africa, I thought I would like to dive with the Great Whites. I had been diving before with the sharks in the Bahamas, but this shark was different. The Great White is big and typically reaches twelve to sixteen feet in length. These sharks have been measured up to 23 feet in length. The Great White weighs around 4,000 pounds and has teeth that are triangular, serrated, and razor sharp. Tests have shown that their bite can exert several hundred pounds of pressure per square inch.

Because of the awesome nature of this shark, we would be inside a shark cage, as it would be dangerous to swim alone in the water with this particular shark. With this in mind, we booked our shark expedition out of Gansbaai, South Africa. Roger had been diving in this area before and knew the details on the location and the diving.

We arrived in Gansbaai the last week of January, a week after our climb of Mount Kilimanjaro. We made all the necessary arrangements and were briefed on shark behavior and the diving procedure. We also met some divers who had just returned from a shark dive. They were very excited about their encounter with the Great White. They had videotaped their trip and it was quite impressive. It showed a huge shark in front of the shark cage. The man who filmed this was so excited about this, he could barely speak.

The next morning we made our way to the dock and boarded our boat. The boat is set up for diving and carries the shark cage on the back deck. The cage itself is round and can hold two people. On the way to the dive site the divemaster gave us instructions on entering and exiting the cage. I listened very carefully to these instructions—I did not want to miss the cage and wind up in the water with a hungry Great White.

There were eight divers on the boat and three passengers. Many people take the boat out to observe the sharks from the safety of the boat. The sea was very rough. This is not that unusual, as this area has waters from the Indian Ocean meeting the waters of the Atlantic Ocean. This makes for very turbulent sea conditions. Half the people on the boat became seasick almost immediately. I have never been prone to seasickness, and I had a TransDerm Scop patch on. This is a prescription patch that is placed behind the ear to help reduce the discomfort of motion sickness. I actually enjoyed the ride. I found the salt air and ocean spray quite exhilarating.

Before long we were slowing down to enter the channel between Geser and Dyer Islands. Immediately I heard the barking of the thousands of seals on the island. Many of the seals would swim alongside the boat. I really enjoyed this experience, as the seals seem to be so happy and playful.

After we were out of the channel, we did not have to go far before the captain shut off the engine. Then a huge head of a shark was put on a line and thrown overboard. This is a controlled method of chumming that attracts sharks to the boat. Unfortunately, after six hours of waiting, no sharks had come into our area. We were not disappointed however, because we knew that the Great White is unpredictable. We would give it another go the next day.

When we awoke the next day, we knew we would not be going out to sea. The dark clouds signaled rain, and the sea was churning as it kicked up white-capped waves. As I mentioned before, the waters off the South African coast can be very treacherous and dangerous. As Roger and I walked down to the dock to check out the conditions, the ocean made its presence known. I could hear the waves pounding the rocks on the shore. I could hear the slamming of the water as it hit the concrete retaining wall, and the crashing of the breakers on shore. I was happy not to be on the boat in these conditions.

The next day the sun was out and the winds were calm. Once again we proceeded to the dock and boarded the boat. And once again the ride to the channel was rough, but since we knew what to expect, it was not a problem.

It was a pleasure to hear the seals again, and to listen to them as they swam to the boat. There are so many of them. The boat slows down as it moves through the channel. Recently, the South African government has restricted the traffic through this area. The boats must have special permission to go through the channel as well as a license for the shark-diving operation.

Soon we arrived at the area where we had been the other day, and once again, the boat crew put the chum line in the water. However, unlike our first day out, a Great White appeared almost immediately. This was a very exciting time, and I could almost hear the thumping heartbeats of everyone on board. My adrenaline started pumping as I listened to the descriptions of the actions of the shark. Roger told me that the dark gray, almost black fin was visible from a long way out.

This was a big shark. It circled the bait about three times in a very methodical manner. Then with lightning speed, the shark moved in on the bait. As it came up out of the water I heard the boat captain say to watch the eyes of the shark. A shark has a membrane, a security eyelid, that closes to protect his eyes whenever he attacks. "Wow!" said Roger, "This shark looks to be at least fourteen feet." "Sixteen," said the boat captain, "Maybe more."

"Time to suit up," said the divemaster. As Roger and I were putting on our wetsuits, the divemaster was giving us our last minute instructions. Basically, I would hold the air tank that supplies the air for both divers. There are two regulators attached to the tank—one for each diver. This meant that I had to be the first one into the cage. I was a bit apprehensive about doing this. Before this trip I had been listening to a TV show about a shark dive like this one. A shark was coming in for the bait and actually slid on to the top of the cage—and then—fell inside the cage!

Fortunately, I made it into the cage with no problems. Soon Roger was dropping in beside me. I gave him one of the regulators and we both dropped down to the bottom of the cage. As we had planned, Roger would need both his hands to operate his camera. I would hold on to the air tank and also hold on to Roger. This was more difficult than it sounds, and as we recall this experience, we compare it to "being inside a washing machine." The cage is attached to the boat and the boat is bobbing up and down with the motion of the sea. Oh, and did I forget to mention that you must also be aware that there is a huge shark right in front of you?

Roger and I did not have any special signal for "sharks," as I did in the Bahama dives. We knew that if we were in the cage, the shark is in close proximity. The boat crew actually drags the chum up to the cage. This is an electrifying experience and not for the faint-hearted. This is excitement times ten. You can feel the presence of the shark. I was making sure all my fingers and toes stayed inside the cage. This was almost more excitement than I bargained for. It was totally awesome.

I then heard three taps on top of the cage. This was the signal from the divemaster to come up out of the cage. He opened the top hatch and we pushed up to the surface of the water. The divemaster told us that the shark had moved away. He told us to hold on to the top of the cage until another shark moved in. Fortunately, we did not have to wait long.

Roger saw the huge fin of a shark and told me to put my mask back on. Then the divemaster told us to go back down to the bottom of the cage. As before, the motion of the cage combined with the awareness of the shark, makes for a very intense experience.

This time the shark circled the boat twice and came back for the chum. The chum was right in front of our cage. While Roger was trying to hold his camera still, in these near impossible conditions, I was making sure my body parts stayed inside the cage.

Again I heard the three taps on top of the cage. The shark had moved off. It was now time for another diver to get into the cage. Roger crawled out of the cage first, and I followed. Quite honestly, I was concerned at this point because I did not want to come out of the cage with so many sharks in the area. It would be quite possible for a shark to breach the water (jump out of the water) as I was trying to get into the boat. Needless to say, I did not waste any time getting out of the cage and on to the boat.

Once on the boat, there is a multitude of feelings. You are glad to be out of the cage and you have an elevated energy level because of the experience. It is much the same feeling I had when I landed after skydiving.

There were over ten different sharks that visited us that day. Some would just circle the boat, while others would wildly attack the chum. These awesome animals should be respected for their place in nature.

They are the top predators in the ocean and have roamed the waters of the world for thousands of years.

I hope these magnificent animals will be around for many more years to come.

Chapter 18

"A large volume of adventures may be grasped within this little span of time of life. by him who interests his heart in everything."
— *Laurence Sterne*

Penguins in Africa

There is a saying that goes, "You can leave Africa, but Africa will never leave you." After my trip to Africa, I certainly know what that means. Traveling to Africa is an experience that you never forget. It is a continent that encompasses so much in its varied cultures, wildlife, landscape, and people. It is a land of wonder and awesome beauty.

I would first like to mention that Africa is a continent with many different countries. I mention this because many people think of Africa as one big country. Many people think Africa is one big jungle. This is definitely not the case. Although there are countries that have jungles in them, there are just as many countries that have major metropolitan areas with modern cities. I am still amazed at the number of people who think wild animals are running around everywhere in Africa. Of course there are areas with an abundance of wildlife, just as there are areas that are like New York City or Chicago.

My first destination in Africa was Johannesburg, in the country of South Africa. The airport was very modern and of course there were no giraffes on the runway or monkeys swinging from the trees. It was in fact, quite like any airport in the United States. The only difference that I picked up on was the language. It has been my experience that many countries around the world are bilingual. Most speak some English as well as their native language, and in many countries people speak several different languages. In Johannesburg, most of the people I talked to spoke English with a British accent. I loved to hear them talk. I also heard people speaking in what I thought was Dutch. I found out later that it was Afrikaans. This is a language spoken by the Afrikaners, who are chiefly of Dutch, German, and French descent. I also heard some people speaking Swahili, which has many different dialects. Swahili is one of the Bantu languages, of which there are over 300 dialects including Zulu.

I stayed at a very modern hotel, which was near the airport. At the time, the U.S. dollar was worth about seven South African rand. I would find out that the American dollar is accepted almost anywhere in Africa, and in many places is preferred over the local currency. The hotel staff were very nice and the food was excellent. Once again, many people believe that the food in Africa is like bush meat, and cooked in primitive conditions. While this can be the case in some remote areas and poorer countries in Africa, the truth is just about any type of cuisine can be experienced in South Africa.

I fell in love with the beautiful weather. When my friend Roger Kyler and I had left Chicago, there was snow on the ground. But the weather in South Africa was about 85 degrees, sunny, and with a nice gentle breeze. The sun felt good on my skin as I sat and listened to the birds that were nearby. I love to hear birds singing and chirping, and South Africa has plenty to listen to.

Roger and I stayed only a few days in "Joburg" as we had planned to climb Mount Kilimanjaro, which is in Tanzania. We would first have to fly up to another African country called Kenya. We landed at the airport in Nairobi, which is the capital of Kenya. On the drive to downtown, Roger told me that the landscape is much like a desert, with some trees and bush grass. The hot and humid weather is typical as the equator runs through the middle of the country. Soon we arrived at our hotel in downtown Nairobi. Nairobi is a large city and is very congested with traffic like any other major city in the world. It reminded me of Chicago.

Since we had to leave for Tanzania the next day, I didn't really get to experience much of the city. However, after our climb of Kilimanjaro we were scheduled to come back to this very interesting country. The next morning we made arrangements to take a shuttle to Arusha. This meant crossing the border to enter Tanzania. We finally secured transportation and were on our way. There were about twelve of us who were packed into an extended minivan. We were packed very tightly up against one another, and our baggage was placed on the roof of the van.

The trip from Nairobi, Kenya, to Arusha, Tanzania, is about 75 miles. The roads are in horrible condition, and have huge potholes that could swallow up most vehicles. From the very start, the driver drove at the top speed of the van. If the van was capable of going 90 miles per hour, then that's the speed he'd drive. It was the only time while I was in Africa that I was afraid for my safety— and you must remember that I was there to climb Mount Kilimanjaro and later, to dive with the Great White sharks!

Along the way there were Masai (also spelled as Maasai) who were moving their cattle across the road. The Masai are nomadic and move about the rural areas of Kenya including the Masai Mara, which is a central area in which many of the Masai live. They are easily recognized by their brightly colored robes. They move from one area to another to find grazing areas for their animals. The driver mentioned that the Masai consider a man's wealth by the number of animals he owns.

The drivers of these "kamikaze vans" would honk their horns for a long time when coming upon a herd of cattle. I do not recall them ever slowing down. I told Roger that I bet every now and then a van collides with a cow. Ten minutes after I told Roger this he said "Gary, there's a dead cow lying out in the middle of the road." Our driver swerved to avoid the cow, and in the process I felt the van go up on two wheels. I thought for a minute that our fate might be the same as the cows.

I was so happy when we arrived at Arusha, Tanzania. I felt as if I should kiss the ground and give the Almighty thanks for getting us safely to our destination. I then remembered we would have to take this shuttle back to Nairobi, so I thought I'd better wait until the return trip. It was great to be in Tanzania and nice to talk with many of the visitors from so many different countries. Arusha is a city that is a meeting point for many of the tourists who are visiting Tanzania's many points of interest. Like us, many are there to climb Mount Kilimanjaro, while others are there to visit the Serengeti National Park and Ngorongoro Crater.

We then boarded a bus to go to the town of Moshi. Moshi is located near Mount Kilimanjaro, and in fact, the mountain can be clearly seen from the town. We stayed at a place called the Keys Hotel. The rooms were small, round concrete buildings with thatch roofs. All the beds had mosquito netting. The dining facility was very nice and served very good food. We decided to spend a couple of days in Moshi to get acclimated to the altitude and to do some hiking around town to get in shape for the climb up "Kili."

We hiked around the town several times. We met many people who were walking along the side of the road. Every day there would be hundreds of people walking to work, going to school, going to town, or just walking down the street to one of the many markets that were along the road. On one of these walks we were joined by about fifteen school children who were playing small, handmade drums. We stopped and talked with them, and they played us a song on their drums. Tanzanians speak Swahili, although many know English. We would greet many with, "Jambo (Hello)," and were often greeted back by, "Hallo." I really loved Moshi and its people.

After our short stay in Moshi, we took a cab to Marangu Hotel. Marangu is a town at the base of Kilimanjaro. Everyone was talking how pretty the landscape was and said that with Kilimanjaro in the near distance, it looked like a beautiful painting. Marangu Hotel is actually several cottages. The grounds are manicured to perfection and the staff is so friendly. It is one of the nicest places I have ever stayed at. I found it interesting that the hot water is supplied by a boiler that is in the back of each cottage. Early in the morning you can hear the workers loading up the firebox and getting the fire going to heat the water. I also enjoyed listening to the blue monkeys playing in the trees. It was like being in some kind of paradise.

We had made earlier arrangements with the hotel to put together our expedition to climb Kilimanjaro. While I go into detail about the climb itself in the next chapter, the experience of getting to the mountain was an adventure in itself. The Tanzanians were so very friendly to us, and although it may be one of the poorest countries in Africa, it is certainly rich in the character of its people.

After our climb of Kilimanjaro, we were on the road again going back to Nairobi, Kenya. The shuttle ride back across the border was a little bit better as we were in a bigger bus. However, it too, was driven to its maximum operating limits.

Once we were back in Nairobi, we decided to visit some of the interesting places in the area. We hired a driver to take a trip to the Nairobi Animal Orphanage. This is a sanctuary for orphan animals of all kinds—elephants, lions, zebras, monkeys, and all other sorts of critters. Many of the animals were here because their families had been killed by poachers. Poaching is still a serious problem in many African countries.

We then took a trip to the Great Rift Valley. This valley cuts through eastern Africa from north to south. The walls of this valley rise to over a mile high in some places, and are 20 to 30 miles wide for much of its length. The Great Rift Valley is home to some of the best farmland in Africa. Going north from Nairobi on the road that goes to Uganda, we would come to our next destination—Hell's Gate National Park in Naivasha.

Hell's Gate National Park is the newest of Kenya's national parks. The park has a wide variety of wildlife such as giraffes, gazelles, zebras, baboons, cheetahs, and many different types of birds. What I liked about the park was that you could walk right out into the field where the animals were. Roger and I left the car and started walking out into a huge field. Roger told me that there was a mother and baby giraffe only a few yards ahead of us. Needless to say, you have to be very cautious and use common sense when approaching animals in an environment such as this. I could hear the giraffes eating leaves off a tree. It was so great.

I then heard a rumbling noise. I could actually feel the ground shaking. A herd of zebras was coming our way. As the giraffes were not moving, we knew we were well out of the way of the herd. On our way back to the car, Roger told me that two warthogs were shading themselves under a nearby tree. We were very close to them, but they seemed to be satisfied with their shade tree. I really liked this park.

The park is known for its volcanic plugs. Upon entering the park there is Fischer's Tower, and at the south end of the park there is Embarta. Embarta is more commonly known as the Central Tower. These unusual structures were formed by semi-molten rock being forced through a crack in the ground. When the lava cooled, it formed the towers. It is a nice place to visit and walk around in. I should mention that some of you have probably seen some of Hell's Gate. It was in the movie *King Solomon's Mines* (starring Stewart Granger), *Magambo* (starring Clark Gable, Grace Kelly and Ava Gardner), as well as the movies *Sheenah, Queen of the Jungle* and *Born Free*. It is a really great feeling to be in such a beautiful place with so much different wildlife. It gives you a real feel for Africa.

After a few days in Nairobi we went back to Johannesburg, South Africa. Then, from "Joburg," we flew down to Cape Town. Cape Town is on the southern tip of Africa. Many who have been there say it is the most beautiful city in the world. It is backdropped by the majestic Table Top Mountain. The mountain gets its name from its resemblance to a huge flat table. Interestingly enough, when it is foggy, the low-level clouds appear to be a tablecloth for the mountain. Of course the oceanside part of the city is equally as impressive. This is where the Cape of Good Hope begins. Cape Town has many modern buildings and overlooks a beautiful ocean harbor. After our climb of Mount Kilimanjaro, this was the perfect place to relax.

Earlier, when I told Dr. Jane that I was going to be in Cape Town, she told me to go visit the penguins. Penguins? In Africa? I now hear this question every time I talk about the penguins. It seems the majority of people think penguins are a cold weather bird. The truth is that although penguins are certainly in the cold climates of Antarctica, most species of penguins are found in warmer climates. It just so happens that in an area near Cape Town are two colonies of the Black-Footed South African penguin. These are adorable birds, although they cannot fly, and stand about two feet tall.

We went to an area called Cape Point. After a short walk to the beach—there they were. Hundreds of penguins. There was a rope that was lying in the sand to mark their nesting area. I sat down on the sand and just listened to these wonderful little creatures. The South African penguins are also known as Jackass penguins because of the sounds they make. There were several of them playing in the surf that was washing up on the beach. As I was sitting there, one of the penguins waddled up to me and laid its head on my thigh. It just stayed there for awhile and then it lifted its head and pecked at my leg. It was as if he was giving me a kiss. He then waddled back to his buddies. It was one of those magical moments in life that you never forget. I could have sat there all day with my new friends.

In time I would have to leave Africa—but Africa has never left me.

The Black Footed South African penguins are found in huge colonies near the south coast of Africa. They are adorable little critters and very playful. *(Cape Town, South Africa)*

Chapter 19

"Nobody trips over mountains. It is the small pebbles that cause you to stumble. Pass all the pebbles in your path and you will find you have crossed the mountain."

—Unknown

"It is not the mountain we conquer, but ourselves."

—Sir Edmund Hillary

Kilimanjaro: The Climb of a Lifetime

On January 25th, 1999, I stood on Uhuru Peak—the summit of Mount Kilimanjaro. It was the climb of a lifetime filled with many challenges—and therein lies the magic. "Accept the challenges, so that you may feel the exhilaration of victory." —General George S. Patton

Mount Kilimanjaro is one of the world's highest free-standing mountains. It rises majestically out of the plains of Africa. Its snow-capped summit seems almost mystical, as "Kili" is located very close to the equator. It is said that climbing Kilimanjaro is the climatic equivalent of going from the equator to the north pole in five days.

My reason for choosing this particular mountain was simple: It is one of the few mountains that does not require any technical climbing. There are trails that lead to the summit. Also, Roger had been on this climb before, and had described the climb in a way that I thought I might be able to do it.

With this goal in mind, I began training a year before I would make the climb. I trained at Champions Fitness Center in my hometown of Rockford, Illinois. I would train on the Stairmaster and the Nordic Trak cross-country ski machine. In addition, I would run three days a week to condition my cardiovascular system and to strengthen my legs.

During the same time period, I began putting together my climbing equipment. For a climb such as this I needed climbing poles, arctic sleeping bag, arctic Gore-Tex parka, thermal underwear, and of course, good socks and a good pair of mountaineering boots. It is important to have proper equipment to have a successful climb.

We also contacted the Marangu Hotel in Tanzania, to put together our expedition. I knew that it would be wise for me to have my own guide. I wanted to have someone with me at all times, and knew this might be a problem if Roger and I had the same guide. I also knew the trail would be steep and covered with ice and snow at the summit. Altogether, our expedition would include Roger and me along with our two guides, a cook, and four porters. The porters carry the firewood, food, water, and arctic climbing gear. These men were from the local Chagga village and knew this mountain very well.

We also decided we would climb the Marangu Route. There are several other routes on the mountain, but this is the most popular one. It is also known as the tourist route because of its popularity. We decided on a five-day climb. Many people take six to ten days on this same route. Taking an extra day helps the climber to acclimate to the altitude. Altitude Mountain Sickness (AMS) can be a very serious problem in the higher elevations of the mountain.

We planned our schedule, and briefly it went like this: Day 1: Marangu Gate to Mandera Hut (8,500 feet). Day 2: Mandera Hut to Horombo Hut (12,100 feet). Day 3: Horombo Hut to Kibo Hut (15,400 feet). Day 4: Kibo Hut to Gillmans Point (18,600 feet), and if possible to Uhuru Peak (19,340 feet). Day 5: Descend from Horombo Hut down to Main Gate. It sounded so easy on paper.

The Climb

After our arrival in Africa, I had a bout with severe jet lag. I had been on a plane for 22 hours with only a two-hour layover in Brussels, Belgium. We spent a couple of nights in Johannesburg, South Africa, and then had to take a six-hour flight up to Nairobi, Kenya. From Nairobi, we took a shuttle bus to Moshi, Tanzania. I had not slept in five days. I think I was apprehensive about this climb. I did not know what to expect. Roger knew I was not feeling 100 percent and told me we could go as far as I felt good about. He said we could turn back at any point. Fortunately, Roger knew that once we started—there would be no turning back. We had trained too long and we had traveled too far.

Day 1

Early in the morning, Roger and I met with the guides and porters for our expedition. The first order of business was making sure we had all the equipment we needed. Once you start the climb, there is nowhere to get items you might need. Although the guides were notified earlier that I was blind, many were curious as to how I would be able to manage on the mountain. The status of blind people in Tanzania is not good. Tanzania is one of the poorest countries in Africa, and the blind do not have many opportunities.

I was introduced to Joseph, who was to be my guide. I liked him immediately. It was obvious that he knew what he was doing, and that gave me confidence and eased many of my concerns about the climb.

153

He was very helpful and attentive right from the start, and he would continue to be to the end of the climb.

We boarded a truck and were driven to the main gate of Kilimanjaro National Park. After registering with park officials, we began walking through the forest area where I discovered the terrain would make it impossible for me to use my mobility cane. Roger's previous climb had been on this same route, but on relatively easier trails; and the trail we were on now was unexpectedly rocky and uneven.

After a while we entered a trail through a dense rain forest. The trail turned to deep mud, and I tripped over many of the exposed tree roots that were on top of the ground. This is not the way I wanted to start the climb. I did not want to become frustrated at the very beginning.

In all the many things I have done—running marathons, karate, judo, skydiving, scuba diving, Japanese swordsmanship—I have never thought of blindness as a handicap. I have been able to deal with being blind in a way that I refer to as maximizing my strengths and minimizing my weaknesses. Basically, I just do the best I can do, and realize there are some things I cannot do. However, on Kilimanjaro, blindness was a handicap. I came to an understanding that I would have to climb this mountain one step at a time.

The word spread quickly of my presence on the mountain. One group of climbers would tell another group, and I was soon the main topic of conversation up and down the mountain. I was told later that some people were actually taking bets on whether or not I would make it to the next hut.

> *"A great pleasure in life is doing what people say you cannot do."*
> —*Walter Gagehot*

We came to a small ravine in the rain forest. It was decided that Roger would go down to the bottom and would help me down. Joseph, my guide, held my other hand as I attempted to descend on the muddy, slippery rocks. About halfway down, my feet slipped from under me and I came down hard. I pinched a nerve in my back and it was very painful. This pain would stay with me until the end of the climb.

154

We eventually came to the Mandera Huts. I was the last one into camp. While most climbers make it to Mandera in three or four hours, it had taken me nine. In a way, this contributed to our success, as we were very slowly acclimating to the altitude. All through the climb, Joseph would repeat, "Pole, pole," which in Swahili means "slow, slow." I did not have any trouble following this advice.

The Mandera Huts are A-frame huts that have bunks for two to six people, or larger huts that house 12 people. Our particular hut housed six on one side of the wall and six people on the other side. It was very basic, a place for your sleeping bag, but under the circumstances, quite comfortable. There was also a huge A-frame hut that was used for the dining facility. I was very tired from the day's climb, and I had no problem getting to sleep. It was my first good night's sleep since arriving in Africa.

Day 2

After breakfast at Mandera Hut, we began climbing through the remainder of the rain forest. Once again it was very difficult for me to manage the exposed roots and muddy trail. Eventually the forest ended and we came into a moorland area. This is much like the prairie grassland we have in the mid-regions of the U.S. The trail we were on had many good-sized rocks and I had to be careful with every step. It is in this area that climbers can first see the top of the mountain. This is because the forest area blocks the view on the first day of climbing.

Again, it took us about nine hours to reach the Horombo Huts (12,100 feet). The Horombo Huts are much like the wooden A-frame huts at Mandera. Climbers going up, as well as climbers who are descending the mountain, use Horombo camp. This is the first chance to hear the stories of those who have made it to the summit. However, since most people do not make it to the summit, many spoke with despair, frustration, and disillusionment. Once again, I was the last one into camp. And once again, I had no trouble getting to sleep.

Day 3

After leaving Horombo Hut, the trail goes over a few rolling hills. These trails had huge rocks on them, much like a dried riverbed. Soon you come into the Saddle, the Highland Desert. This is a vast alpine desert, which most people describe as "looking like the surface of the moon." It is very important to wear a wide-brimmed hat and use plenty of sunscreen as it is very easy to get sunburned in these conditions.

For me, this was the easiest part of the climb, as the trail was much like walking on a country road. However, the Saddle is where most people begin to experience some form of Altitude Mountain Sickness (AMS). The symptoms can include headache, loss of appetite, nausea, vomiting, and extreme fatigue. Personally, I think this is where all those long hours at the gym paid off.

As we walked along the trail leading to Kibo Hut, we passed Mount Mawenzi. Some say this sister mountain to Kilimanjaro is one of the most beautiful sights during the climb. After several hours on this trail, Roger said he could see Kibo camp. However, it would still take us over two hours to reach it.

Kibo Hut (15,400 feet) seems a dismal place because climbers are dealing with the altitude. It is very hard to get to sleep because you know you will be getting up at midnight to make an attempt on the summit. Many climbers turn around and go back down at this point. Here, it is easy to understand why the success rate for climbing to the summit is so low. This is where you must summon up all the physical and mental strength you have. Only those with determination will make it past Kibo Hut. However, of those, only a few will reach the summit.

> *"Live your life each day as you would climb a mountain. An occasional glance toward the summit keeps the goal in mind, but many beautiful scenes are to be observed from each new vantage point. Climb slowly, steadily, enjoying each passing moment; and the view from the summit will serve as a fitting climax for your journey."*
>
> *—Harold F. Melchert*

Day 4

We were awakened by Joseph just before midnight. We got our cold weather gear together to prepare for our summit attempt. There are three reasons why the climb to the summit is made during the early morning darkness—1) the scree (the pebbles and sand mixture found near the summit) is frozen and you get traction, 2) the guides want you to be at Gillmans Point by early morning so you can see the sun come up over Mount Mawenzi, and 3) if people could see what they had to climb, they probably would not do it.

Most people have flashlights or headlamps to help them navigate the trail. I held on to the strap on Joseph's pack and used one climbing pole for balance. It is interesting that batteries have a tendency to not work so well at this altitude, and many climbers have to deal with the darkness. Strangely, I somehow took comfort in the fact that many of the climbers would now understand why I was always the last one into camp.

Climbing to the summit is very difficult because it is very steep. The loose scree is treacherous as you take one step, and slide back three. It becomes very frustrating and physically demanding. The cold is also a problem, and many climbers turn back because they are not prepared to deal with the arctic conditions at this altitude. My water bottle froze completely solid.

We made it to Gillmans Point (18,600 feet) around 7:30. It was definitely a struggle for me because I actually had to crawl up and down several huge rocks and boulders. Joseph would place my feet down on the rocks and then repeat this process until I was over the rocks. I was almost completely exhausted and felt like I had after finishing a marathon. But in this case, it was like someone saying, "It's not over with yet…there is still a long way to go."

Gillmans Point is considered to be the "top of the mountain." In fact, once you make it to this point you are eligible for a certificate stating that you made it to the top. Most people turn back at this point. However, the summit is another one or two hours of steep climbing on snow, ice, and loose gravel.

After a brief rest, Roger and I decided to go to the summit. At this point it becomes an exercise of mental determination to push through total exhaustion. The thin air was causing me to breathe rapidly and I was becoming fatigued. Joseph would actually pull and push to help me climb the very difficult terrain. Roger told me later that he did not want me to panic, but that about two feet away from me was a drop-off of over 500 feet.

We were both fighting altitude sickness, pushing the limits of pain and exhaustion. We would move one step at a time along the rim of this majestic extinct volcano, surrounded by the towering ice glaciers and snowfields. It was very windy and cold, but we just kept climbing. And then…we were there.

Uhuru Peak (19,340 feet) is the summit of Mount Kilimanjaro. It is the highest point in Africa. It had taken us about two hours to reach this point after leaving Gillmans Point. I was totally exhausted. It is hard to describe, as it was the best feeling in the world and also the worst. The climb to the summit had taken its toll on me physically and mentally. But spiritually I knew I had accepted the challenge, and now I stood on the top of the mountain. As I reflect back on this moment, it has since served to strengthen me. Many of us must face challenges every day, and it is how we accept and overcome these challenges that makes us who we are. A person's life can be like climbing a mountain. With determination and a positive attitude, we must keep moving and do the best we can do. The experiences along the way, and the people we meet on the journey will give us strength to make it through the tough times.

We spent about 15 minutes on the summit while Roger took some pictures and we rested. Joseph wanted to get us moving as the wind was picking up—and Uhuru Peak is no place to be when the wind starts whistling as it comes over the top of the mountain. It sounds rather eerie and at the same time quite beautiful. It is as if the spirit of the mountain is acknowledging your presence.

For me, the descent from the mountain was just as difficult as the climb up. Walking down the crater rim was extremely hard because there were some long drops to the path. We then headed back toward Gillmans Point, going straight down the mountain by "surfing" the scree. This is done by stepping down and sliding several feet, slowing down with the other foot, and then quickly repeating this process. This would actually be fun to do if I had not been totally exhausted. I would in fact, slide several feet, sit or lie down for a few minutes, and repeat this process until we made it back to Kibo hut.

When we made it back to Kibo, we had about an hour to recover before we made our way back to Horombo. I was extremely tired and still breathing rapidly. I told Roger that I was too tired to make it down to Horombo. I lay down on the bunk and immediately went to sleep. When Joseph came in to wake us, I told him I did not know if I could make it back to Horombo camp. He assured me that this is common and that I would get stronger as I moved down the mountain.

I was amazed that with almost every step through the Highland Desert I was feeling stronger. I would need this strength, because as soon as we were out of the Saddle, our trail back to Horombo can only be described as hellish. It was a series of big rocks and some that could be labeled as boulders. It was a trail that I will never forget as long as I live, and it seemed to take us a lifetime to reach Horombo.

Day 5

The descent down the mountain was as difficult as the ascent. I still had to deal with the rocky terrain of the grasslands and the mud and roots of the forest. It seems that during the descent is when most people get blisters. I think this is due to the sliding motion and the angle of the foot in a downward motion. I was lucky in this regard and did not get any blisters during the climb. I was also elated because I had made it to the summit.

From Horombo we made it down the mountain to the park entrance. The truck from Marangu Hotel was at the gate, waiting to take us back to the hotel. As soon as I got back to our cabin, I jumped in the shower. After five days without a bath or shower, this was a heavenly experience. Hot water was now a luxurious experience. After putting on some clean clothes, it was now time for the expedition celebration.

The first order of business is the tipping of the guides, cook, and porters. Roger and I both agreed that we had been taken care of very professionally. We knew that it was a team effort that made ours a successful climb. I was especially grateful to my guide, Joseph, who helped me make it every step of the way. While we were very generous in compensating our expedition, I think the bond that was developed through this experience, is something that money cannot buy. While we had a huge amount of respect for the hard work of our expedition, Joseph said the porters had gained respect for me, too. He said that the porters had watched as I would just keep moving over the rough terrain. In fact, the porters had been telling the porters of other expeditions of my progress and my determination. In broken English, Joseph said that I was an inspiration to them and that they would tell others in their village about me. He then said, "Gary, you are (a) strong man—in here." He then took my hand and put it on my heart. "Kili (was) hard for you, (but) you strong on Kili."

Joseph then gave Roger and me our certificates for making it to the summit. We then toasted each other for a successful climb. Then we toasted to Kili. It was a great feeling. Standing in the shadows of Kilimanjaro knowing I had been to the top. It was the experience of knowing I had pushed myself both physically and mentally beyond the limits of endurance into what I call the realm of accomplishment.

> *"The reward of a job well done is to have done it."*
> —*Ralph Waldo Emerson*

The porters and guides gathered around and started singing the Kilimanjaro song. They clapped their hands and sang in a harmony that one can only hear in Africa. That night I dreamt about the mountain, and came to an understanding that this beautiful mountain would be with me forever.

> *"The future belongs to those who believe in the beauty of their dreams."*
> —*Eleanor Roosevelt*

Uhuru Peak (19,340 feet). The summit of Mount Kilimanjaro. It was never the goal to reach the top of the mountain. It was always the goal to reach inside myself.

Chapter 20

"Success: To laugh often and much, to win the respect of intelligent people and the affection of children, to earn the appreciation of honest critics and endure the betrayal of false friends, to appreciate beauty, to find the best in others, to leave the world a bit better, whether by a healthy child, a garden patch, or a redeemed social condition; to know even one life has breathed easier because you have lived."

—Ralph Waldo Emerson

Gary Haun

A Vision for the Future

Martha Washington once said that misery or happiness depends not so much on our circumstances, as it does on our disposition at the time. I wish I could have met Martha. I'm sure I would have liked her. Her words have inspired me and helped me to look at difficult situations with the best possible disposition.

Sometimes life can be difficult. There are no guarantees of happiness. No free passes on contentment. Sometimes it seems that when we're walking in the valley, it's hard to even think about reaching the mountaintop. Despair and depression are the stormy weather of our emotional and mental well being. This cold rain and violent thunder can shake the foundations of our souls, and I'm no stranger to the rain.

I think the best we can do is just try to do the best we can. I mean it. Don't take life too seriously. Darkness will consume us if we let it, but the light within can and will show us the way. Sometimes we can make a situation worse by surrounding the situation with negativity. But there's no magic in facing adversity—it comes down to you and your attitude.

The price of a good attitude and a bad attitude are exactly the same. It's a matter of choice. However, the costs of choosing the wrong attitude are very high. Do the math. Connect the dots. I know life gets hard sometimes. Believe me, you aren't the first person to walk down a rocky road. It's just that sometimes you feel that you're all alone in the world, and that no one understands what you're feeling. Well, how can they? They aren't walking down the road with you. But if you let them, their spirit will hold your hand and help carry your bags along the way.

It's not my intention to speak for others. It seems there's too much of that going on already. I don't speak for other blind people, just as one sighted person can't speak for all of the sighted. It's not my place to encourage others to do what I have done. Not at all. Shark diving and climbing mountains may not be for everyone. Each one of us is unique, but I'd like to encourage others to enjoy life by doing things they like best.

I think it's important to listen to the birds. To feel a summer breeze. To feel the sun warm on your face on a spring day. I think the simple things in life help make things less complicated. It's possible to get more enjoyment out of life, but we have to let it happen, and we have to be open to it. The beauty of being happy is within us, but like the beauty of the rose, it can be choked out by the weeds of negativity. But only if we let it.

It's sad to think of all the people with unfulfilled ambitions and long lost dreams. Don't let your dreams stay lost. Get up and find them again. Rekindle the flames of the passion you once had for new directions and exciting ideas. I used to dream about flying through the air; but now after skydiving, I sometimes dream about other people who are dreaming about flying through the air. I suppose I want them to feel the same way I felt.

I remember as a child, looking through a kaleidoscope and changing the view with every turn of the wheel. Upon reflection, it seems that with each new day, we're making another turn of the kaleidoscope. Constantly changing, new shapes, new colors—a whole new perspective. I can't remember what my view of life was yesterday; I only look forward to the newness of each day. Each new day is like a canvas waiting for the artist to fill it with color—and I'm that artist, and I'm the one who will make it come alive.

When I gaze through the telescope into many tomorrows, I see lots of things I'm going to be doing. Dog sledding, hang gliding, diving with the Great White sharks of the Great Barrier Reef, visiting the emperor penguins in Antarctica—and I know my vision and the reality will become as one because I have the desire to make it so.

Keep your own dreams and wishes alive and make them happen. Choose to be positive. Face adversity with strength and you will become stronger. I know life has its difficult moments, and it seems that some people are dealt more bad cards than others. But it's important to keep playing, and the good cards will come your way. Being happy simply by wanting to be happy is your wild card.

The toughest times in darkness are those times when the light is weak within, so surround yourself with the candles of many good friends. Let the light of these candles guide you when the path is dark. The glow and the warmth from these candles will bring a peaceful feeling to your soul.

It's my wish that this book will help bring you vision—maybe a certain clarity or a newly defined focus. I hope it might add a new panoramic view to your future, and I hope your reflection on life's waters will be everything you want it to be. Stop looking over your shoulder and focusing on that empty canvas. Let tomorrow be Day One, a new day of not gazing into the crystal ball, but of actually being in that future vision. All it takes is Vision From the Heart.